A DAUGHTER OF THE KING

Lisa A. Saunders

WESTBOW
PRESS
A DIVISION OF THOMAS NELSON
& ZONDERVAN

Bible Verses & Notes

23 For all have sinned and fall short of the glory of God. Romans 3:23*

INTRODUCTION

I asked myself, "How do you want to be remembered?"

As a good wife?

As a good mother?

As a good NICU nurse?

Think on these questions as they pertain to your life and occupation. Additional space is provided for notes as you read and referenced verses are included. Those verses with a star (*) show up more than once. Unless otherwise noted, all verses are taken from the Holman Christian Standard Bible (HCSB). A section is provided for lengthy passages and additional verses noted in a discussion. Some topics have multiple verses listed as references. In this instance one may find these passages noted on a preceding or following page. I believe this takes care of all housekeeping chores. So, let us begin.

Anyone can be remembered as a good wife, mother, or professional. Only you and I, as believers and followers of Jesus Christ, will be remembered as daughters of the King!

As daughters of the King, we are to be treated as Christ commands we treat others and as He treated others: with unconditional love and mercy, and as heirs to God's kingdom.

Let us now begin the journey to become daughters of the King.

We are all born with an innate desire to be loved. After having worked as a registered nurse in the neonatal intensive care unit for over thirty years, I can honestly say all infants, no matter the circumstances surrounding their birth, have the same basic needs:

Bible Verses & Notes

nutrition, warmth, and most importantly love. On this we can all agree.

Where does this need or desire for love arise? As a follower of Jesus, I believe God designed us with a space specifically to be filled with His love. For each of us, this area may change its location at various times throughout our lives. Nevertheless, it remains open and ready to be filled. How do we fill it with God's love in a permanent way?

- We confess all are sinners and understand we cannot follow enough rules or do enough good works to do away with our sins so that we may approach the presence of God (Romans 3:23*).
- We accept Jesus Christ as the only Son of God, born of a virgin and sent to live as a man to minister to others, teach about this love, die for our sins, and defeat death through His resurrection (John 3:16–17*). We must humbly pray and ask Jesus to become our Lord and Savior.
- We daily take up His cross while repenting of our sins, meaning our minds do not want to think of them again, and we spread the story of Jesus to others (Luke 9:23; *Mark 16:15–16*).

I believe this area exists and demands to be filled. Most of us, as generations living in a world of instant gratification, attempt to fill it with worldly idols or gods. Food, medications (both legal and illegal), alcohol, media, worldly knowledge—these last for only a minute.

The area was not intended to be filled with these, so they are but a temporary space occupying relief—much like a gas bubble in an infant's tummy: there is no nutritive value, and it provides no growth and leaves them miserable and hungry in a short time. Unless we as caregivers release that space and fill that tummy with what was intended to provide comfort and growth, the infant will cry and cry!

Now, where does that space reside in you? Only you can answer this. For me, it has relocated from my digestive system to the knowledge section of my brain to the pituitary gland within my brain (that exceedingly small, bothersome part that directs our sexual thoughts and desires). Can we say it follows a path directed by stages of development and maturity?

The bottom line is only when I filled it completely with God's love—meaning I placed God on the throne of my heart by developing a relationship with Jesus—could I say I was truly satisfied.

What does Jesus tell us He is?

- the Bread of Life; we will hunger no more (John 6:35)
- the Water that quenches all thirst (John 4:13–14)
- the Way, the Truth, and the Life; the only pathway that will lead us to God (John 14:6)

By confessing myself a sinner, accepting Jesus as my Savior, and repenting of my sins, I am an heir to God's kingdom and a daughter of the King (John 1:12-13; Titus 3:7).

Bible Verses & Notes

35"I am the bread of life," Jesus told them. "No one who comes to Me will ever be hungry, and no one who believes in Me will ever be thirsty again. John 6:35

13Jesus said, "Everyone who drinks from this water will get thirsty again. 14But whoever drinks from the water that I will give him will never get thirsty again — ever! John 4:13-14

6Jesus told him, "I am the way, the truth, and the life. No one comes to the Father except through Me. John 14:6

12But to all who did receive Him, He gave them the right to be children of God, to those who believe in His name, 13who were born, not of blood, or of the will of the flesh, or of the will of man, but of God. John 1:12-13*

7so that, having been justified by His grace, we may become heirs with the hope of eternal life. Titus 3:7*

Bible Verses & Notes

OVERVIEW

This book and Bible study is meant to help us understand our place as women in God's kingdom. We become followers of Jesus Christ, believing in Him as God's only Son. We believe that He was sent as a sacrifice for our sins, knowing that through His death and resurrection, He provided us the gift of eternal life. Adding to this a personal relationship with Jesus, built on daily walks in His Word and daily talks with Him, changes us from worldly women to daughters of the King.

Within this study, we shall compare being a daughter in God's kingdom to aspects of being a member of the British monarchy, which will serve as a likeness to the world in general.

The first session reviews how one becomes a member of the royal family of God and compares this to how one becomes a member of the British royal family, a more worldly view of royalty. We will examine the methods used biblically to choose kings and how one becomes an heir to God's kingdom, comparing these to the means by which one becomes British royalty. This session ends with the introduction of the Comparison Chart, which will be used throughout the entire book or study. The Comparison Chart, which has a suggested format provided, along with the questions given at the end of each session, called Discussion Points, can be used by the reader to help develop a better understanding of the topics discussed within each session and allow reflection upon how God is speaking to them through those topics. Those using the book in a group format should have a Comparison Chart for their class and use the Discussion Points to promote feedback during class.

The second session involves readers taking an in-depth look into the coronation ceremony—those of the Old Testament, the New Testament, and the British monarchy. Readers may find it enjoyable to view footage of Queen Elizabeth II's coronation ceremony. For group participants an actual coronation ceremony makes a refreshing end to this session. The "Helpful Hints" page includes items useful for planning a group's ceremony.

The third session focuses on our duties as daughters of the King. As changed women, we are to think of ourselves differently, present ourselves as godly women, and treat others using the examples given by Jesus in His ministry. The discussion will include the gift of the Holy Spirit and how best to tap into its power and the power of prayer. Again, as a means of comparison, we will look at the expectations and traditions placed on members of the British royal monarchy. This session will end with use of the Comparison Chart and Discussion Points.

The fourth session explores how we, as daughters of the King, should be treated by others. As godly women, we should command respect for our heavenly Father and for ourselves. We will research how to earn respect in biblical terms and apply those behaviors to our own circumstances. For class participants, this session will end with role playing for those attendees comfortable with doing so. For readers, they will find it beneficial to write out their own scenarios and solutions using the Discussion Points as guidelines.

The fifth and final session considers the price of royalty. What does the world say we have sacrificed as daughters of the King? What does the Bible say about sacrifice and persecution? What do we gain or lose? We shall analyze a British sovereign's sacrifices to the crown and consider what are our own crowns that we may sacrifice for.

There is a sample Certificate of Adoption & Completion provided. Like a diploma one receives upon graduation, this demonstrates to others the dedication, hours of study, and accomplishment the reader or participant submitted and now has achieved upon completion of all sessions. It also notifies the world

Bible Verses & Notes

Bible Verses & Notes

of one's adoption into the Kingdom of God. My prayer is that each reader or group participant would have the opportunity to print their own certificate. It is also my hope and prayer that each reader and group participant would be able to purchase or receive a Crown of Faith as another token of recognition. This crown could be a small charm worn as a piece of jewelry or kept close at hand (such as a key chain ornament) and also serves as a reminder of one's inheritance and duties as a daughter of the King.

HOW DOES ONE BECOME A MEMBER OF A ROYAL FAMILY?

29And if you belong to Christ, then you are Abraham's seed, heirs according to the promise. Galatians 3:29

5Listen, my dear brothers: Didn't God choose the poor in this world to be rich in faith and heirs of the kingdom that He has promised to those who love Him? James 2:5

8In other words, it is not the children by physical descent who are God's children, but it is the children of the promise who are regarded as Abraham's offspring. Romans 9:8

*6Teach a youth about the way he should go; even when he is old he will not depart from it. Proverbs 22:6

4Therefore, the Lord Himself will give you a sign: The virgin will conceive, have a son, and name him Immanuel. Isaiah 7:14

3For I passed on to you as most important what I also received: that Christ died for our sins according to the Scriptures, 4that He was buried, that He was raised on the third day according to the Scriptures. I Corinthians 15:3-4

Once upon a time, a young girl dreamed of becoming a princess. She watched all the Disney movies about princesses. She knew all their names and could sing all the theme songs. She even asked for crowns and princess costumes for gifts, to wear on Halloween and when playing dress-up. While growing up, she watched Miss America pageants and practiced receiving her crown and bouquet of flowers.

Is this not how most fairy tales begin, or at least modern-day fairy tales? I doubt the Brothers Grimm had to check with Disney or Pixar regarding copyright infringements.

While growing up in the Deep South during the sixties and seventies, many young girls dreamed of wearing a crown at some time in their lives. Whether as the high school homecoming queen or a court member, the queen of a peanut or peach festival, or even the queen of a festival honoring the boll weevil. A beetle that ruined the Alabama cotton industry during the 1920's and caused farmers to become better stewards of the land by using crop rotation. Only in the South are "pests" so honored for their use by God to help educate humans! If her family were of a certain financial and, shall we say, historical status within the local community, she would even aspire to be a legacy queen of a Mystic Order or Crewe, such as those found in New Orleans, Louisiana; Mobile or Montgomery, Alabama; or many other cities within the South and maybe our entire country, at her debutante ball during her "coming out" season. Yes, we still have those here in the Deep South. Please understand that even as I am using these in a lighthearted manner, by no means would I disgrace or lessen their importance to those families that were so kind to include me as a guest and provide me an opportunity to attend such events as a young teen. Many families continue to support these as part of long-held traditions, and many young ladies have benefited in their pursuit of advancing their education because of pageants and family memberships within these groups.

My point is many young girls have felt, as I have, that they were too fat or too thin, that their hair was either too curly or too straight, that their clothes were too homemade looking, or that their families were not rich enough for them to deserve a crown of any kind.

I felt this way until I heard about and understood there was a kingdom in which all are welcome and can become children of the King (John 1:12-13*; Galatians 3:29; James 2:5; Titus 3:7*; Romans 9:8[New International Version]). I learned of the kingdom and its King, God, as a young child. What my parents could not provide in worldly terms, they certainly did so in spiritual ones. My mother took me to church Sunday morning and evenings, even when my father (a long-haul trucker) was working. She made sure I could participate in all children and youth activities. This gave me that foundation spoken of in Proverbs 22:6*, which I would lean on as I grew up.

Sad to say that, even though I became a child of God, accepting Jesus as my Savior at an early age (around six or seven years of age) one Easter morning along with the rededication of my father, I did not fully grasp the concept of what it means to be a daughter of the King until I was an adult and had made many mistakes. That is why God has placed this Bible study, this project, on my heart: to help other young girls and women—all women, to be honest— understand their potential, their responsibilities, and their place in God's kingdom.

As believers and followers of Jesus Christ, we can all wear a crown of faith. The first step we must take is that leap of faith, that bold step out of the world's hold. By faith we accept Jesus as God's only Son, sent to earth to live as a human (John 3:16–17*), being born of a virgin (Isaiah 7:14), and dying on the cross, a most cruel and torturous death for our sins (1 Corinthians 15:3-4). You see, we cannot enter the throne room of our heavenly Father, our Abba (according to *The Complete Jewish Study Bible,*[1] an original Aramaic word that became incorporated into ancient Hebrew and translated into a most affectionate way of saying Father or Daddy), as our sinful selves (1 John 1:5). Therefore, Jesus had to become the ultimate sacrifice. In His perfection and being sinless, He took upon Himself our sins; yes, even those sins of generations not born and therefore not committed. By faith we are saying that through His death on that cross, we now have access to the throne of God when we pray (Hebrews 4:16). Beyond the death of Jesus, we also accept on faith His resurrection—that after three days in the tomb,

Bible Verses & Notes

5Now this is the message we have heard from Him and declare to you: God is light, and there is absolutely no darkness in Him. I John 1:5

6Therefore let us approach the throne of grace with boldness, so that we may receive mercy and find grace to help us at the proper time. Hebrews 4:16

Bible Verses & Notes

12For our battle is not against flesh and blood, but against the rulers, against the authorities, against the world powers of this darkness, against the spiritual forces of evil in the heavens. Ephesians 6:12

it was found to be empty that early "Easter morning" by His friend Mary Magdalene (John 20:1–16). We now say death as the world knows it has been defeated.

After faithful acceptance comes repentance, meaning utmost regret or remorse for an action or behavior. We have concluded we are sinners, one and all (Romans 3:23*), and we understand that because of our human nature, we continue to sin. But God, through Jesus, has supplied us an avenue for true repentance. This means we confess, or openly say to God in prayer, the sin. As the queen of rationalization, I have found that if you do not say it out loud, it does not become a truth. Praying about the sin gives it validity and helps me, through the assistance of the Holy Spirit, develop a plan to ensure I will not continue that behavior. That is repentance.

We have faithfully accepted Jesus, repented, and taken steps to not continue behaviors leading to our sins, and now comes our best defense against those forces, which will begin working earnestly to make our lives a discredit to our newly announced faith (Ephesians 6:12). This step is our daily walk in God's Word, the Bible. We must begin developing a relationship like no other, with Jesus. I began to appreciate this type of a relationship with Jesus while participating in the Bible study by Henry Blackerby, *Experiencing God*.[2] As our Sunday school class worked through that study, I allowed myself to become open to God. I involved myself as if it were one of my nursing courses in college. However, instead of simply memorizing material for a test, I figured out how to apply it in my everyday life. I finished that study a changed and more mature disciple or student of Christ, which is my prayer for each and every one of you who reads this book or partakes in a group discussion of this study.

One of the many concepts I embedded in my brain from *Experiencing God* was how to verbalize a definition of how the Holy Spirit interacts within our lives. We all remember the Trinity: The Father, Son, and Holy Spirit. I know you may be thinking, *Didn't she say she grew up in the church, attending all those Sunday school classes, Girls in Action classes, and What Baptist Believe classes? What was she doing during all those sermons, those two-a-days?* OK, so, maybe I was not totally engaged in the content of the sermon, and maybe once I became of age to sit in the balcony, all those notes were not necessarily biblical. But hey, cut a gal some slack. I do have a medical condition: I have narcoleptic tendencies. And yes, that little topic could become a whole chapter itself!

Nevertheless, if someone had asked me to explain how the Holy Spirit fits into my life, let's just say my BSN degree would reflect the BS part—babbling syntax. Bet you thought I was going to say a more worldly phrase, correct? Using what *Experiencing God* taught me about the Holy Spirit, I am attempting to give you my version of the more eloquent writings of Mr. Blackerby and others. As a parent, I have bought my child the most sought-after gaming device on Cyber Monday, getting the best deal ever. It arrives and is in perfect working order. I have it well hidden and ready for Christmas morning. In the meantime, my child sees a commercial for the Slam Bam Thank You Ma'am Gun—remember, we are in the South. It has a soft-ammo propelled launcher and shoots water at an unheard-of distance, all while glowing in the dark.

Oh, my mercies, that is all I hear now: "Please, please, please can I have the Slam Bam gun, Momma? I promise I will be good and do whatever you ask." We have all said it and heard it. Now, I have already purchased this gaming device, which had been the hot ticket item for months prior. And no, we cannot afford both. Plus, we all know this gun will hold their attention only that day, parts will get lost, and the batteries will run out, leaving us with the conclusion of which is the better gift in the long run.

Without spoiling the surprise, I must guide my child's thinking away from the "latest, greatest, make your life oh-so-fun" toy to what is waiting for him under the tree. Do you get where we are headed with this? The Holy Spirit knows what awesomeness God has planned for us. Even though, like that child, we keep praying, "Please, please, please," if we are quiet and still, the Holy Spirit will guide us toward wanting what is already waiting behind God's door! I do hope and pray this makes sense to you now and as we continue discussing the Holy Spirit.

In *Experiencing God*, I also learned the relationship we are forming with Jesus should be like that of our first love. Think back

16All Scripture is inspired by God and is profitable for teaching, for rebuking, for correcting, for training in righteousness. II Timothy 3:16

Bible Verses & Notes

10Finally, be strengthened by the Lord and by His vast strength. 11Put on the full armor of God so that you can stand against the tactics of the Devil. 12For our battle is not against flesh and blood, but against the rulers, against the authorities, against the world powers of this darkness, against the spiritual forces of evil in the heavens. 13This is why you must take up the full armor of God, so that you may be able to resist in the evil day, and having prepared everything, to take your stand. 14Stand, therefore, with truth like a belt around your waist, righteousness like armor on your chest, 15and your feet sandaled with readiness for the gospel of peace. 16In every situation take the shield of faith, and with it you will be able to extinguish all the flaming arrows of the evil one. 17Take the helmet of salvation, and the sword of the Spirit, which is God's word. 18Pray at all times in the Spirit with every prayer and request, and stay alert in this with all perseverance and intercession for all the saints. Ephesians 6:10-18

to those days, ladies. For some it may be just a few days back, and for others it may seem a lifetime ago. But you can remember your first love where you had to know everything about that person. You talked with them in the morning and at night. It was as if your life was consumed by them. I recall my sons having their first loves and saying to them, "Oh, my mercies. Why, your Daddy and I are married, and we don't even talk to each other that much!" We could dive deep and chase that squirrel for a hot minute, as we say here in Alabama. The understanding is this: Jesus is to become our all-consuming, "start and end the day" person. He is that person we want to know everything there is to know about, that person who becomes our BFF.

For unbelievers and those not committed to following the gospel of Jesus, the evil one's job is done. Once we take on the cross and begin living according to the teachings of Jesus, the evil one gathers his forces and goes to war. That war includes daily battles in our lives that we must recognize and be ready for.

Because I grew up in the Deep South and blessed with three sons, I will use football analogies, such as Jesus used farming and Galilean weddings in His parables and teachings. We must use the Bible as our playbook to formulate our game plan to defeat the evil one. Through God's inspired writings (2 Timothy 3:16), we have an instruction manual for life, for battles, for discipline of others and ourselves, and for any problem needing a solution. The most difficult part of this step, this relationship development, is this: for those of us grasping the concept later in life, we must make it a priority in our daily routine. And yes, as my mother used to tell me, if I am pointing one finger out, how many are pointing back at myself? That would be three. Therefore, God has me writing this book, this study, not only for you but for myself as well. Please keep that in mind and do not think I have it all figured out, because this little Southern belle is far from perfect and has much to learn herself. As I would tell new nurses or student nurses, "If you ever feel like you have nothing else to learn, then you might as well grab a big glass of sweet tea and a rocking chair, sit on your porch, and wait for the Second Coming of Jesus. 'Cause honey, ya got nothing left to do but wait at that point. As far as I know, there is no retirement plan verse in the Bible."

Let's get back on track. This routine must include putting on the full armor of God each day (Ephesians 6:10–18*). Just as football players need all their equipment—helmet; shoulder, hip, and knee pads; and braces, along with other protective devices—we too must gird ourselves for the "flaming arrows" of the evil one, or else we become targets for pain and injury. But with that full armor of God, we can resist evil and be prepared to take our stand in the world as daughters of the King.

With all three pieces in place—acceptance of Jesus, repentance of our sins, and daily taking the Cross and walking in faith with Jesus (Luke 9:23*)—as children of God, heirs to His kingdom, and daughters of the King, we can now wear our very own crown of faith.

LET US SAIL ACROSS THE POND TO LOOK AT BRITISH ROYALTY

My husband and I began watching Masterpiece Theater and British media productions many years ago. He has a love for American history, and after a couple of Air Force Reserve tours in and around England, he found a desire to learn more about his family heritage and British history. By no means has he found any leaf or link to the royal family through his genealogy research, but he has discovered his family's line did originate in Scotland. Oddly enough, we discovered my father's family originated in England, and my mother's family was from Ireland. This has led to bookshelves in our house with numerous volumes on the British monarchy and its history. As I began compiling the information God was installing in my brain circuitry for this study, a comparison to the British royal family ensued because it depicts a more worldly view of royalty. As a result of this gleaned knowledge of Britannia, or all that is British, each session will include the discussion topic from a biblical standpoint and then relate that topic to equivalent information as it pertains to the British monarchy.

Bible Verses & Notes

To become a member of the British royal family or its lineage, one of the following must occur:

- One is born into the line of succession. This is just as Jesus was born of the lineage of King David (Matthew 1:1), or the Jewish Nation was God's chosen people through the children of Abraham (Genesis 12:1–3).
- One moves into position after a death. The death of Jesus allows our entrance into the throne of God (Luke 23:44–46); once the curtain of the sanctuary was torn in the temple, all could enter.
- The current monarch resigns his or her position.
- A royal marriage takes place.

This royal family would appear very inclusive. If not by birth, to become a member, one traditionally could not be a commoner. That means Mom and Dad must have a title that is of royalty, and not just Mr. or Mrs., or even Doctor or Esquire (a lawyer). One must attend the proper school and all the accepted functions, which probably does not include the fall festival at church, the Road to Resurrection reenactment at church, or (especially in the Deep South) a college football game! I think even being the homecoming queen at your favorite college or the president of the most sought-after Greek house on campus would not suffice. What's more, the fact that your great-grandmother, grandmother, mother, and you were crowned queen of the debutant ball at a country club would not prompt an invitation to ride or stalk the elk at Balmoral Castle or dine at Sandringham House (just a couple of the houses this family owns). Can we agree this is a group whose ranks are difficult to penetrate? But as history demonstrates, they are easy to fall afoul of. One wrong remark, one wrong outfit, or one association with an outsider, and you will find your invitations to those social gala events are becoming rarer.

But in God's kingdom, we have His promise found in Isaiah 41:10 of His help and His holding on to us "with My righteous right hand" (HCSB). I do not know about you, but for me, my crown of faith and God's righteous right hand are far more enticing than any worldly, royal piece of jewelry or gemstones.

Now, let me introduce the Comparison Chart, remember a sample format is located near the end of the book. This will be used throughout the book as we discuss and compare God's kingdom to that of the British monarchy and worldly kingdoms. For those participating as a group, there may be a large chart for use in the classroom or leaders may provide individual copies for those attending.

Bible Verses & Notes

Session 1
Discussion Points

1. Briefly trace the family tree of Jesus, using Matthew 1. Highlight names you recognize and note their significance.

2. For the Comparison Chart, list the steps one takes to become a daughter of the King and those listed for becoming a British royal family member.

3. Which steps seem more difficult, and why?

4. Which family appears more supportive of its members, and why?

CORONATION CEREMONIES: BIBLICAL AND BRITISH

Bible Verses & Notes

6 *6And it came to pass, when they were come, that he looked on Eliab, and said, Surely the LORD's anointed is before him. *7But the LORD said unto Samuel, Look not on his countenance, or on the height of his stature; because I have refused him: for the LORD seeth not as man seeth; for man looketh on the outward appearance, but the LORD looketh on the heart. 8Then Jesse called Abinadab, and made him pass before Samuel. And he said, Neither hath the LORD chosen this. 9Then Jesse made Shammah to pass by. And he said, Neither hath the LORD chosen this. 10Again, Jesse made seven of his sons to pass before Samuel. And Samuel said unto Jesse, The LORD hath not chosen these. 11And Samuel said unto Jesse, Are here all thy children? And he said, There remaineth yet the youngest, and, behold, he keepeth the sheep. And Samuel said unto Jesse, Send and fetch him: for we will not sit down till he come hither. 12And he sent, and brought him in. Now he was ruddy, and withal of a beautiful countenance, and goodly to look to. And the LORD said, Arise, anoint

Some may recall viewing the actual coronation ceremony of Queen Elizabeth II, the current British monarch, sovereign, and ruling head of state. Of course, this would have been seen on a black-and-white television that probably had only three or four channels (depending on where one lived), and it used antennas known as "rabbit ears" to facilitate receiving the signals for those channels. This was the first world-televised coronation ceremony of a British monarch, and the year was 1953.[3]

I have watched her crowning only in movies and special series, such as *The Crown*.[4] When my husband and I watched this series for the first time, the episode involving her coronation[5] impressed me with the majesty and reverence associated with the service, in particular the part of the episode in which she recalls rehearsing the ceremony with her father, King George VI.

As God was using the Holy Spirit's guidance to help me design this book and study, I began thinking of the ways in which God anointed His kings, such as David and Jesus, and how He anoints us as His children.

This research helped me realize how closely aligned the British ceremony is with those seen in the Bible.

In 1 Samuel 16:6–13 (King James Version)*, we find the description of David's initial anointing as a king. He was chosen by God and handpicked by the prophet Samuel from the sons of Jesse. As mentioned in the Comparison Chart, this denotes the earthly lineage of Jesus as being directly from King David.

We find Samuel, following God's instructions regarding uncovering the new king of Israel among the sons of Jesse, from Bethlehem (1 Samuel 16:1–4a). God charged Samuel to fill his horn, a ram's horn that was hollowed out and used to carry the oil used for anointing or calling someone into service or used as an instrument one might blow into as a means of calling others into action. Are we catching God's drift with this whole horn thing? Either way, what God is telling Samuel in this passage, in terms we understand, is what I have been known to tell new nurses facing tough times: "Pull up your big girl panties. Let's clean up the spilled milk and move on, buttercup!" You see, Samuel was upset over the present king's governing abilities. Sound familiar?

He was spending more time fussing and crying over the spilled milk, as we say Down South. In an answer to Samuel's prayers, God was leading him to a new king; he simply had to heed the call to action. Samuel takes his horn of oil and sends the invite to "Jesse and Sons," requesting their attendance at a sacrificial peace offering ceremony.

To begin with, Samuel looks at the eldest son and, based on his appearance, decides (in our modern terms), "This has to be the one" 1 Samuel 16:6* (KJV). But God, as we see in 1 Samuel 16:7*(KJV), states His rejection of this son and says to Samuel not to look at just their appearance. God does not see people through human or worldly eyes, meaning looks, financial status, where they live or go to school, or even who their parents are. He sees people's hearts. He sees their motives, their inner attitudes and thoughts, and their inner pains and scars. This can be a welcomed relief as well as a hit on the head by a two-by-four, as we say here in the South.

Keep in mind I grew up in an old-money Southern town and graduated from what some might call an "elite" private school. Now to attend this school my father would work extra hours as a diesel mechanic and my mother worked two jobs. For you see, I lived on one side of the train tracks (yes, we still have those in the Deep South, and they divide the city into "parts of town"), while most of my classmates lived on the other side. Many times, I relied on this verse when the "rich kids" (in my mind) got whatever they asked for. To me, they already had everything. But God knew their hearts, their hurts, their pain, and their home lives. If I had known their circumstances—and I did later learn some of them—I would have realized they lacked things I had, such as a family that loved me no matter what I looked like, or the grades I made, or my tryout results.

Finally, Samuel had to make Jesse bring all his sons, because the Lord had chosen from none of those present. You see, Jesse had left his youngest son, David, tending sheep. He did not feel him worthy to attend the ceremony, much less suitable to be chosen by God as king. In 1 Samuel 16:12*(KJV), when David arrives, we see God tell Samuel to get up and anoint this one, "for this is he"

Bible Verses & Notes

him: for this is he. 13Then Samuel took the horn of oil, and anointed him in the midst of his brethren: and the Spirit of the LORD came upon David from that day forward. I Samuel 16:6-13* (King James Version)

1The Lord said to Samuel, "How long are you going to mourn for Saul, since I have rejected him as king over Israel? Fill your horn with oil and go. I am sending you to Jesse of Bethlehem because I have selected a king from his sons." 2Samuel asked, "How can I go? Saul will hear about it and kill me!" The Lord answered, "Take a young cow with you and say, 'I have come to sacrifice to the Lord.' 3Then invite Jesse to the sacrifice, and I will let you know what you are to do. You are to anoint for Me the one I indicate to you." 4Samuel did what the Lord directed and went to Bethlehem. I Samuel 16:1-4a

Bible Verses & Notes

16Simon Peter answered, "You are the Messiah, the Son of the living God!" Matthew 16:16

29"But you," He asked them again, "who do you say that I am?" Peter answered Him, "You are the Messiah!" Mark 8:29

20"But you," He asked them, "who do you say that I am?" Peter answered, "God's Messiah!" Luke 9:20

41He first found his own brother Simon and told him, "We have found the Messiah!" (which means "Anointed One"). John 1:41

3Then Mary took a pound of fragrant oil — pure and expensive nard — anointed Jesus' feet, and wiped His feet with her hair. John 12:3

29They twisted together a crown of thorns, put it on His head, and placed a reed in His right hand. And they knelt down before Him and mocked Him: "Hail, King of the Jews!" Matthew 27:29

17They dressed Him in a purple robe, twisted together a crown of thorns, and put it on Him. Mark 15:17

38how God anointed Jesus of Nazareth with the Holy Spirit and power, and how he went around doing good and healing all who were under the power of the devil, because God was with him. Acts 10:38 (NIV)

(KJV). Samuel took the oil from his horn and did as God said, in the midst of David's father and brothers (1 Samuel 16:13* KJV).

Moving into the New Testament, we observe God's ultimate Anointed One, the Messiah, His only Son, Jesus. According to the glossary of Hebrew words in *The Complete Jewish Study Bible*,[6] *Mashiach*, found in passages throughout Hebrew writings, can be translated as Messiah or Christ in English. It literally means "anointed" or "an anointed one." If you look at the Greek writings of the New Testament, you will find the use of *christos*, which has been translated into Christ in English and also means "anointed."

Therefore, even though Jesus, according to Matthew 16:16, Mark 8:29, Luke 9:20, and John 1:41—those disciples writing His story—became God's earthly Messiah, He was not necessarily anointed as a king of the Old Testament nor as one would be today. What God anointed Jesus with, as we discover in Acts 10:38(New International Version), was the Holy Spirit and power, both of which provided Him what was necessary for His ministry. We do find in John 12:3, toward the end of the earthly ministry of Jesus, that Mary, the sister of Lazarus and a close friend of Jesus, anointed His feet with oil, wiping them with her hair. Mary did this as a sign of her devotion and love of Jesus as her friend, the one who raised her brother from the dead, and her Messiah. She performed an anointing in public, demonstrating to all present that Jesus is "the Anointed One."

Jesus did receive a crown, but it was one of piercing thorns, and it was placed harshly and cruelly on His head as a form of ridicule at the time of His crucifixion and death (Matthew 27:29; Mark 15:17). Yes, at this time He was given a purple robe, a sign of royalty, and a sign was placed on His cross in Hebrew, Latin, and Greek saying, "Jesus the Nazarene, King of the Jews" (John 19:19-20). Hardly the ornate, beautiful, sacred, or even touching ceremony seen in the anointing of David. Nor can it be compared to that of the kings and queens of England.

Yet I dare say that crown of thorns has provided more hope in times of struggle and saved more people for eternal life in heaven than any four- to five-pound bedazzled, bejeweled headpiece worn today. No monarch can say the words spoken by Jesus in Revelation

22:13, "I am the Alpha and the Omega, the First and the Last, the Beginning and the End" (HCSB).

For those of us who become believers and followers of Christ, our anointing or making sacred in a ceremony can be likened to one's public profession of acceptance of Jesus and subsequent baptism, as Jesus details in (Matthew 28:19*), and as Peter instructs in (Acts 2:38* and 1 Peter 3:21) (NIV). For now, as stated in (1 Peter 2:9–10) (NIV), we are a chosen group, a royal priesthood, a part of a holy nation that is now a possession of God.

Jesus did away with the old standards set by the ruling religious leaders (Galatians 2:15-16), those ways in which humans attempted to overcome sin through sacrifices and following rules passed down from the priests. This method offered no measure in which humans could attain worthiness suitable to enter the throne room of God. Nevertheless, with the sacrifice of Jesus, we no longer require an anointing of oil to be recognized as daughters of the King.

Once we receive the gift of the Holy Spirit, spoken of in (Acts 2:38*) and (1 John 2:27), our true anointing has occurred. With the Holy Spirit comes our power, our means of discernment and decision making, and our intercession when praying. Like Jesus, we can use this power to change our world to bring hope, love, and light where darkness has brought depression, sadness, and addiction.

Within a biblical coronation, a covenant or a strong, solemn agreement is formed between two parties. It joins them so tightly that they subsequently become identified as one. At the core of this covenant is a change in their relationship. One must promise to do or not do an action for generations to follow. The parties call upon God to bind them and hold them accountable, making it a serious offense if the covenant is ever broken.[7] What types of arrangements made today can we equate to this? Right off the top of my head are the marriage vows. On a lighter note, due to living in the Deep South, we can also recall those talked-about feuds between families, kinfolks, and neighbors. You know, back when Cousin Bubba allegedly stole Cousin Billy Bob's prize huntin' dog! I think to this day, those two are still feudin' about the promise they made growing up, signed in spit and blood, that they were to

Bible Verses & Notes

19Pilate also had a sign lettered and put on the cross. The inscription was: JESUS THE NAZARENETHE KING OF THE JEWS. 20Many of the Jews read this sign, because the place where Jesus was crucified was near the city, and it was written in Hebrew, Latin, and Greek. John 19:19-20

19Go, therefore, and make disciples of all nations, baptizing them in the name of the Father and of the Son and of the Holy Spirit. Matthew 28:19

38"Repent," Peter said to them, "and be baptized, each of you, in the name of Jesus Christ for the forgiveness of your sins, and you will receive the gift of the Holy Spirit. Acts 2:38

21and this water symbolizes baptism that now saves you also—not the removal of dirt from the body but the pledge of a clear conscience toward God. It saves you by the resurrection of Jesus Christ. I Peter 3:21 (NIV)

Bible Verses & Notes

9But you are a chosen people, a royal priesthood, a holy nation, God's special possession, that you may declare the praises of him who called you out of darkness into his wonderful light. 10Once you were not a people, but now you are the people of God; once you had not received mercy, but now you have received mercy. I Peter 2:9-10 (NIV)

15We who are Jews by birth and not "Gentile sinners" 16know that no one is justified by the works of the law but by faith in Jesus Christ. And we have believed in Christ Jesus so that we might be justified by faith in Christ and not by the works of the law, because by the works of the law no human being will be justified. Galatians 2:15-16

2 7The anointing you received from Him remains in you, and you don't need anyone to teach you. Instead, His anointing teaches you about all things and is true and is not a lie; just as He has taught you, remain in Him. I John 2:27

be best friends forever and that dog was to be shared during huntin' season. (All names have been changed to protect the innocent.)

OK, let's get back to business at hand. The biblical coronation covenant was made between the Lord, the man chosen to be king, and the people. The people would be the Lord's people, the King would be the Lord's king, and the king himself made a covenant with his people to govern according to God's law, in a fair and just manner. Therefore, as His disciples, we should look at making a covenant with Jesus as part of our rebirth. What would that agreement look like or say? To me, this presents a remarkably interesting question that each of us must answer.

For me, my covenant would start out as follows.

- I promise to profess Him as my Savior, the Son of God. I am not ashamed of Jesus and the cross.
- I will begin a daily walk with Him to establish the relationship He desires and deserves.
- I will follow His teachings and obey the call to serve when asked.

These are but a few of the actions I feel are needed for me to form that solemn agreement one could call a covenant. Next comes the writing of specific steps to achieve each of these. For only then can we honestly say our covenant has started to become that promised agreement.

YOUR INVITATION TO THE CORONATION OF A BRITISH SOVEREIGN

In *The Crown*, season 1, episode 5, we see a young Elizabeth rehearsing a part of the British coronation ceremony with her father. We learn the Archbishop of Canterbury, the leader of the Church of England, presides over and conducts the ceremony. It is held at Westminster Abbey, the church of all churches in England. Kings and queens have been crowned here since 1066.[8] Royal weddings take place here, and believe it or not, actual worship services are held there each Sunday. Her father tells her the people becoming kings and queens must be willing to make a promise they cannot break (where have we seen this before). The two characters, father and daughter, role-play the part of the ceremony known as the anointing. He tells her one must be anointed to become king or queen. He then explains the procedure. It involves using holy oil to "transform" the person being coronated. Once the oil touches them, they become in direct contact with the divine. They are bound to God and forever changed. I am sensing déjà vu, how about you? He tells her it is the most important part of the ceremony. It is so special and sacred that it cannot be viewed by others. Her father allows her to play the part of the archbishop, and he explains the steps in the anointing.

First, the oil is placed on the hands; I see this as symbolizing our service to God and to others. Next, the archbishop moves to place oil on the chest; I look upon this as the binding of one's heart to the love of God, others, and myself. Last, the oil is placed on the head, which to me represents wisdom. Solomon, himself a great king, prayed for wisdom and discernment so that he may know the best ways to govern (1 Kings 3:9–12). He then tells Elizabeth she has just participated in a process observed by kings, priests, and prophets as they too were anointed. What are your thoughts on the symbolism of the hands, heart, and head?

Elizabeth asked her father about the actual crown he would wear. She learned it weighed approximately five pounds; it really weighs four pounds, twelve ounces and is solid gold.[9] But as her father, soon to be King George VI, reminds her, its symbolic weight is far greater. Are we seeing a parallel between the symbolism he speaks of and that of the crown of thorns? What was the weight of the crown worn by Jesus as King of the Jews?

A few interesting elements I noted while viewing this episode included the amount of bowing and kneeling taking place before their throne. It is just as we are taught to bow or kneel out of reverence and respect when praying, as we ourselves are going before the throne of God. I also noted within the British ceremony, they speak of the sovereign as having been chosen by God. We too have now become chosen members of God's kingdom (James 2:5). What also became apparent was their use of the word

Bible Verses & Notes

9So give Your servant an obedient heart to judge Your people and to discern between good and evil. For who is able to judge this great people of Yours?"

10Now it pleased the Lord that Solomon had requested this. 11So God said to him, "Because you have requested this and did not ask for long life or riches for yourself, or the death of your enemies, but you asked discernment for yourself to understand justice, 12I will therefore do what you have asked. I will give you a wise and understanding heart, so that there has never been anyone like you before and never will be again. I Kings 3:9-12

Bible Verses & Notes

5Listen, my dear brothers: Didn't God choose the poor in this world to be rich in faith and heirs of the kingdom that He has promised to those who love Him? James 2:5

2 Do not be conformed to this age, but be transformed by the renewing of your mind, so that you may discern what is the good, pleasing, and perfect will of God. Romans 12:2

transformation, meaning the person arrives in a mere human form but leaves as a royal sovereign with godlike qualities. Now, we do not go quite that far with our thoughts on the transforming of ourselves once we become followers of Jesus. But Romans 12:2* does instruct us to be transformed. In that we renew our minds and not conform to the ways of the world, so that others can see God through us by the way we live our life and treat others.

This completes our analysis of the coronation ceremony. Use the Discussion Points to complete your Comparison Chart and, if possible, view the coronation ceremony of Queen Elizabeth II. Group participants may find it to be a time of reflection and fellowship to engage in an actual ceremony once the Discussion Points have been reviewed. Suggestions for a ceremony may be found on the page noted as Helpful Hints.

Session 2
Discussion Points

1. What similarities can you find between the two ceremonies, the biblical and the British coronations?

2. What differences do you see?

3. What parts of the British ceremony did you find meaningful?

SESSION 3

A ROYAL JOB DESCRIPTION– BIBLICAL ROLES & DUTY TO THE CROWN

At this point, we have established our inheritance as daughters of the Most High King and possibly attended our own coronation ceremony or viewed an actual ceremony. Now, we should note the following: What is our role as children of God, as faith-filled women?

I believe God designed women for extremely specific reasons. That's pretty obvious, right? After looking at the first two chapters of Genesis, we can envision God as He is making a dwelling place for humankind, and then as he makes man. Man was to be the overseer, the caretaker, the one to maintain all God had created up to this point. Now, if you will allow me some biblical, comical, and literary latitude, I will explain my theory as to the next sequence of events. My hypothesis is based on life as an aunt of three boys, as a mother of three boys, and as a wife. I have quite a few of these hypotheses—do we see another book on the horizon?

God, in His infinite wisdom, realized man needed help. Man was getting bored, as men so often do, and as a result he began having fun with the naming of a few of the animals, such as aardvark, hippopotamus, or spiny lumpsucker.[10] When God heard of these names, He called to man and asked to see such creatures. Of course, man, being a man, could not find them. At this point God became weary and made woman to be man's helpmate, organizer, multitasker, and finder of all things. Seriously, though, ladies, do you not agree with this theory?

Back to factual biblical roles for us as daughters in God's kingdom. If ever I need a reference for my function as a godly woman, wife, or mother, I look to Proverbs 31:10–31. My feeble attempt to supply a condensed version of this passage can be found later in this session. Within these verses, I find my responsibilities toward my husband, my profession or occupation, my family, my finances, and my part in helping others. I see there are times for laughter, and I praise the Lord for those things, as well as for loving instructions. I remind myself of the loving aspect when instructing and do not act out of anger or when I am hurting.

Let me take a quick sidebar and explain my memory verses and life rope. When I mention these, it means there was a season in my life during which my faith was being strengthened, or as in

Bible Verses & Notes

2Consider it a great joy, my brothers, whenever you experience various trials, 3knowing that the testing of your faith produces endurance. 4But endurance must do its complete work, so that you may be mature and complete, lacking nothing. James 1:2-4

Bible Verses & Notes

James 1:2–4, I was in the middle of a trial, which God was using to make me a better and stronger person. But between you and me, amid those seasons I have a difficult time finding joy. What I do find are memory verses, those promises from God drilled into my brain during my childhood at vacation Bible school or discipleship training or found when I am using the Bible or another faith-based study guide to carry me through this season. Each of these verses form knots in my life rope, which I use to pull me along through that season, another season, or pass along to someone during a stressful time in their life. I have found having these memory verses to rely on help tie and secure the knots in my life rope. Meaning those parts of the rope used to aid in climbing or rescuing. My life rope, as I call it, is used to pull myself out of pits of darkness, depression, doubt, and fear. To strengthen the rope, make more strands in it, or add more knots to use for my hands when climbing, I use those memory verses of God's promises and the ones learned during those seasons in my life when through a trial my faith became stronger. This project has provided numerous additional knots for me and hopefully, prayerfully will do so for you as well.

A memory verse for me is Proverbs 31:30, "Charm is deceptive, and beauty is fleeting, but a woman who fears the Lord will be praised" (HCSB). I know you will think I am off my rocker for saying this, but I find such comfort in this verse. God is letting me know that when someone is blessing my heart or calling me precious, they may not always do so in a truthful spirit. Meaning charming words can be deceiving. As well as I'm sorry to say, glamour and beauty, no matter the number of alterations and injections, is fleeting—but a faith-filled woman, walking with God will be praised! Just writing about this verse makes me hold my head higher, sit up straighter, and smile. I have made another knot in my life rope right now. What about you? Now, let's get back to those roles God inspired the writer of Proverbs 31 to give us gals.

This writer gives us some pretty daunting duties:

- ensure the trust of our husband
- work with hands that enjoy the tasks they are performing

- make sure the household has appropriate clothing, food, and shelter within budget
- keep the body strong so we can continue to provide for our family and others
- make sure the household has provisions for hard times, so we can then help others during those times
- let strength and honor be our clothes so that our family is held in high esteem within the community
- laugh when the time is right
- provide wise counsel to other women and friends
- become role models for our children

All of which reflect our actions and faith as women who love God and are followers of Christ.

In addition to these, let us not forget Matthew 28:19-20, which tells us as followers and disciples of Christ, making us heirs to the kingdom, that we have the duty to go out into the world and teach others about Jesus.

Now, let's get real, ladies. The woman described in Proverbs 31 and the one Jesus needs to spread His story would appear to be a superwoman. She alone could not accomplish those jobs or come close to that bold, courageous, evangelical, angelic picture we may have in our minds. But God has given us another promise and memory verse: Mark 10:27. Jesus tells us that by ourselves, things are not possible, but with God, all things are possible.

From the passage in 1 Samuel, in which we discussed the coronation of David as king, we can find concepts noteworthy for us in researching our duties. Let me go back to the part of that story in which God talks about looking past a person's outward appearance, whether it be richly adorned or tattered and torn, and viewing the person's heart. 1 Samuel 16:7b* (KJV)

Who could have imagined that humble, young shepherd boy having the Spirit of the Lord rush upon him and being chosen to lead a nation and an army for God (1 Samuel 16:13a English Standard Version)? I need to stop right here, close my eyes, and attempt to conceptualize "the Spirit of the Lord rushing upon" someone (English Standard Version). Can it be compared to that

27Looking at them, Jesus said, "With men it is impossible, but not with God, because all things are possible with God." Mark 10:27

13Then Samuel took the horn of oil and anointed him in the midst of his brothers. And the Spirit of the Lord rushed upon David from that day forward. I Samuel 16:13 (ESV)

14But now thy kingdom shall not continue: the LORD hath sought him a man after his own heart, and the LORD hath commanded him to be captain over his people, because thou hast not kept that which the LORD commanded thee. I Samuel 13:14 (KJV)

Bible Verses & Notes

16Turn to me and be gracious to me. Give Your strength to Your servant; save the son of Your female servant. Psalm 86:16

16Lord, I am indeed Your servant; I am Your servant, the son of Your female servant. You have loosened my bonds. Psalm 116:16

12For the word of God is living and effective and sharper than any double-edged sword, penetrating as far as the separation of soul and spirit, joints and marrow. It is able to judge the ideas and thoughts of the heart. Hebrews 4:12

16All Scripture is inspired by God and is profitable for teaching, for rebuking, for correcting, for training in righteousness. II Timothy 3:16

feeling one has during childbirth, when those labor pains are so excruciating that we just cannot take another moment, but then the staff show up for our epidural, and it works? Or compared to that feeling a bride has when the doors open, and her groom sees her for the first time in her gown, knowing she will soon be his wife? Or maybe that truly awesome time when your child says, "Momma, I want Jesus in my heart!" Use a blank page to write some examples of what you think that might be like.

As I mentioned earlier, even David's own father felt him so unworthy that he did not bring him to the banquet, much less did he think of him as being good enough to be chosen by God as king. But God had sought for Himself a man after His own heart, one whom He knew would make that promise, that commitment, that covenant with Him to follow Him and lead His people (1 Samuel 13:14 King James Version). Now, let us pause for a minute with a glass of tea or a cup of coffee and think about this. The phrase "a man after His own heart" means God's heart. So, girls, what do you think God's heart is like? We need multiple pages for this — whatcha think? I feel God's heart is so big that it holds all our tears, our prayers, our wants, and our dreams, as well as the love He has for us all. It also holds all the love for past and future generations, and of course all those pets waiting on us in heaven. I know I missed some aspects that y'all can add. Feel free to discuss your thoughts on God's heart in your next group meeting or with someone you trust as a mentor or faithful friend.

What made David so special in God's eyes? What made him a man after His own heart? David speaks to us in Psalm 86:16 and Psalm 116:16 about his mother, calling her God's servant. Because David uses this phrase, I feel he was given the foundation by his mother, while growing up, to become the person God sought. Hearing of God's love and seeing a mother demonstrate a strong relationship with God helped make David the special man he became. That leads us to see another duty we have: to ensure our children, and all children God places in our circle, hear of God's love, see us as we form our relationship with Jesus, and see how we treat others. We are to help them form a love for Jesus, giving them a foundation that will not fall or fail them in their future. Proverbs

22:6* is another memory verse for me, and it gives me the promise I need for my own children as I struggle with their decision making. Can I get an amen from you ladies on this one?

We use the Bible for our benchmark (how about an amen from the MBAs?), for our policy and procedure manual, knowing it is sharper than any two-edged sword and its writings are inspired by God for teaching and helping others, as well as ourselves (Hebrews 4:12; 2 Timothy 3:16). For example, simply by going over what is known as the Sermon on the Mount found in Matthew 5 and Luke 6, we can find Jesus giving us a lesson on ethical behavior or our code of conduct. He speaks to those who are blessed by their circumstances in life and those who should be "woeful" of theirs. As for those of us, His children, we are given our duties as we interact with others.

For instance, we are to love and pray for our enemies, for those who do us wrong or treat others wrongfully. Let me stop for a minute and contemplate the difficulty I and you may have had with this one over the years, especially when it came to those enemies and their treatment of my children, or children in general. For reasons that might constitute another book, I can forgive (but probably not forget, because I am a female) those who hurt me. But hurt my children or another child, and I become loaded, target locked, and ready to fire. Remember that I am from the South, and we are gun totin' folks. Actually, I do not own a gun—why should I when everyone else in my family does? I feel I can do more harm with my streetwise wit, mouth, prayer, and common sense. Plus, I would probably be like one of my most beloved characters from television, Miss Suzanne Sugarbaker from the show *Designing Women*.[11] Yes, she carried a gun, but she had to empty her designer bag to find it.

OK, back on track. We are not to judge others, unless we want to be judged by God using our own standards. I for one have been known to be quite the catty little sorority girl in my day, and no, I would not want those standards turned around back to myself. What say you, my girlfriends? Are you always dressed for success when you drive up to the local one-stop-shop parking lot? You know, where we buy our ammo, our fishing bait, our dress for Sunday school, and our ham for Easter lunch? I know I'm not!

34Then Jesus said, "Father, forgive them, because they do not know what they are doing." Luke 23:34

22"I tell you, not as many as seven," Jesus said to him, "but 70 times seven. Matthew 18:22

Bible Verses & Notes

31By faith Rahab the prostitute received the spies in peace and didn't perish with those who disobeyed. Hebrews 11:31

12Looking all around and seeing no one, he struck the Egyptian dead and hid him in the sand. 15When Pharaoh heard about this, he tried to kill Moses. But Moses fled from Pharaoh and went to live in the land of Midian, and sat down by a well. Exodus 2:12,15

Last, but not least, we are to forgive. Christ gives us the ultimate example in that while dying on the cross, He asked His Father in heaven to forgive those who had wronged Him and performed this act (Luke 23:34). As part of His teachings, when asked how often we should forgive someone, He stated this: seventy times seven, meaning each time we are wronged (Matthew 18:22). Keep in mind once we forgive someone, we first are obeying what we have been taught, and this opens the door for God's forgiveness of our sins; second, we release any hold this bitterness is placing on us by the evil one, and joy can now enter our hearts. I realize we are all thinking, "These duties are quite daunting. How could little ol' me ever be able to do them?" I agree. But God, so many times throughout the Bible and in life, picks the most unlikely or least thought of by the world to do His work. He picked David, the youngest and a lowly shepherd boy with many sins as an adult, to become one of the greatest kings and to be a part of the earthly lineage of His Son, Jesus. He picked Rahab, a woman of sordid reputation (as we say Down South), to help the spies sent by Joshua when setting up the Promised Land, and as a result He protected her family from death (Joshua 2:1–24; Hebrews 11:31). He sent a murderer who had been banished from his homeland, Moses, to save the Israelites (Exodus 2:12, 15; Exodus 3:7–10). He sent a baby, Jesus, to save the world (John 3:16–17*).

One of the most beautiful examples I recently discovered outside of those within the Bible is that of Josef Mohr. In 1816, the Austrian priest penned the words that would become the most popular Christmas carol in the world, "Silent Night."[12] Josef was born in 1792, the illegitimate infant of a seamstress. His father left them both, and he grew up in extreme poverty, but his mother sacrificed what money she had to have him baptized. In so doing, she opened the door God had built for Josef to meet the choirmaster of that church. This man recognized his talent and helped him obtain an education. Josef entered the priesthood, and while serving in a cold and improvised alpine village, he found comfort in the picture of Mary and her Son, Jesus, in his church. This picture led him to write a poem, "Stille Nacht," in which he portrays that still night that changed the world. Two years later, with friend and church organist Franz Gruber, who wrote the melody, he brought to life the carol. I have condensed the story greatly, but God used these two men—one who, without the love of his mother, would have been unknown at the time of his death—to give the world today (some two hundred years later) a cherished and well-known work of art. I am tearing up just writing those words. So, ladies, what does God have planned for each of you? Why does God pick those least thought of to do His work? He does this so we and others can see and understand His power, His might, and His grace, and so all the glory for that work becomes a testimony for Him, not humankind. He also uses it to strengthen that unlikely person's faith in Him. The bottom line in all of this is it is our duty to say yes when we are called for a mission.

We may not think of ourselves as teachers, church leaders, speakers, writers, or whatever pathway we feel the Holy Spirit is nudging us toward. Yet based on biblical promises, when we say a few magic words, "Yes, Lord," He will help us become great, just as He helped those mentioned earlier and so many others.

Denying ourselves the opportunity to obey a calling to serve while trusting God's promises can cause us to experience mental and physical health issues. Take this fool's advice on this one, please. Personally speaking, this book is a prime example. If I did not heed God's call, then between 2:00 and 4:00 a.m., I would be awake and having a conversation with the Holy Spirit!

To sum it up, a basic duty as daughters of the King lies in transforming ourselves by renewing our minds (Romans 12:2*). By doing so, the world will see a change in our hearts, our outlook on life, how we handle stress, and the way we relate to others. We can now become a reflection of God's Word. We have the gift of the Holy Spirit, the part of the Trinity providing that extra prodding toward God's will. We have a new process for decision-making using prayer, discernment, and faith rather than making them on a whim, on our own after phoning a friend, or even worse after accepting worldly advice that probably does not have our best interest in mind. Just like with the British monarch who walks out of Westminster Abbey, the world now sees the newest member in God's kingdom: you.

JOB DESCRIPTION FOR A BRITISH SOVEREIGN: ONE'S DUTY TO THE CROWN

Speaking of our British counterparts, we examined in session 2 that as part of the British coronation ceremony, the soon to be monarch makes a covenant that cannot be broken in the presence of all those present at the crowning. This includes their immediate family members, government leadership, and church leadership. This promise is to serve the Crown. What does that mean? Not the almost five-pound, solid gold, bedazzled headpiece worn during ceremonies but the institution it represents, such as the Church of England, the country and its people, the monarchy or the family line, and the governing bodies that may legislate or make rules for the people to follow. Are we seeing the same type of setup as the kings of the Old Testament and their covenants—those made between the Lord, the chosen ruler, and the people. The British sovereign promises, in the sight of God, to be that chosen ruler, to honor the Church of England, and to rule according to standards set by both the people (represented by Parliament) and the church.

This concept of duty involves traditions and roles passed down from centuries ago. A few of these include the following.

- Whom to marry—A marriage is not always based on love but on what is best for king and country.
- How to perform when speaking in public—This includes diction, verbiage, and presentation of the content written for you. In the past, ladies of the court would have their hands tied together with rope and secured around their waists. This teaches one to stand and speak without using one's hands.
- How to always dress—This applies during formal events as well as playtime events. This one is particularly important because there are dress codes for both adults and children.
- Subtle communication—One of the more interesting items I found in my research of this topic centers on the queen and her famous purse. Not only does it serve as a means to carry a weapon, a small tube of lip gloss, or a cell phone,

but for the queen, it is a means of communication. She uses it to send signals to her staff, depending on which arm she moves it to, such as "Stick a fork in me; I am done with this conversation," or if placed on the table, which means "time to call it a night, and dinner is officially over."

- How to sit—One is to sit with a straight back, not touching the back of the chair, with hands in your lap and legs crossed only at the ankles. Knees and ankles are held together and placed slightly to one side. This one has been passed down through many genteel Southern charm schools and sorority rush pledge classes.[13]

From media outlets, news channels, movies, documentaries, books, and interviews detailing recent royal family rumormongering, we have discovered once one becomes a royal, friendships are closely monitored. One need not associate with commoners because they really would not understand you, nor you them—and come on, ladies, they really are not one of us. But Jesus ministered to those most unwanted, feared, and despised. He reminded us hospitals are for the sick, not the well (Matthew 9:12-13) and all are considered sinners (Romans 3:23*).

Royals, especially those within the immediate ruling family, are told where to live. Even though it is a palace, it is not the dwelling place you picked out with your spouse, and it does not necessarily contain your family furniture, knickknacks, that heirloom velvet Elvis picture passed down from Aunt Susie Rae, or that masterpiece known as *Dogs Playing Poker* you inherited from Gramps. What I mean are those items that personalize it for you and your spouse. I read an interview given by Princess Dianna regarding her initial impression of Buckingham Palace. She felt it was dark, drafty, and lonely. She stated when she opened curtains, she was immediately told to close them, or photographers with zoom lenses would take compromising photos. How miserable. No sunshine, no clouds, no sunrise, and no sunset—those displays of God's majesty that let us know He is there. No wonder those folks have so many issues and need to have so many houses.

Bible Verses & Notes

12But when He heard this, He said, "Those who are well don't need a doctor, but the sick do. 13Go and learn what this means: I desire mercy and not sacrifice. For I didn't come to call the righteous, but sinners." Matthew 9:12-13

Through the life of Princess Dianna, we see even a royal, fairy-tale princess can have the same struggles with rejection, feelings of unworthiness, and low self-esteem that many women have today. So many people struggle with these feelings that they subject themselves to forms of self-abuse causing some manner of pain, in the form of cuttings, eating disorders, or allowing others to abuse their bodies just to try to feel something.

As a member of the royal family who is in line to occupy the throne, one essentially has no choice as to occupation, classes at school, and even name. You are named according to your lineage, meaning what is chosen for you to be known as or the names you will bear. To put this in Deep South terms, you cannot be named after your momma's favorite mee-maw's granddaddy, or her best friend from high school, or her college roommate—much less Gramp's favorite huntin' dog!

Now, I am not saying all those rules and regulations for the royal family are bad or totally unheard of in my neck of the woods. Many of them could be found in any old *Emily Post's Etiquette*, should the local antique shop have one. We all have been asked by our mothers or whoever sent us out the door to school, "You are going to wear that?" We have been told to sit and stand straight, not to ramble when we speak, and by all means watch out whom we associate with because they can influence our thinking and what others think of us.

In conclusion, the duties and traditions associated with being a royal place your needs and those of your family second to those of the Crown. Your behaviors, your actions, and your life become focused on maintaining and preserving the sanctity of the monarchy. But at what cost?

Food for thought: taken to the extreme, preserving the Crown could mean idolizing an institution, and that can become detrimental to a person, but in essence, should we not show such devotion to our faith in Jesus? That is something to put on the table for discussion.

Normally the sovereigns place their duties to the Crown above family, love, relationships, basically themselves and anything else. As we continue through this book and study, let us think about this: What is our crown? What are we willing to place above all else in our lives? Is Jesus our Crown? Are we ready to take self out of the equation and let Jesus occupy the throne of our hearts, minds, souls, and strength? Or if we open our checkbooks, our calendars, and our notepads on our phones, or if we think about what we just viewed on any form of media in the past twenty-four hours, do we see idols that allow worship of God or those that show worship of the world? For me, this hits home. I have found myself placing my family, my work, my recreation time, and even my church duties above those times I should have been walking closer with Jesus. So yes, we all need to think about this and make some changes in the way we prioritize our time, our relationships, and our everything.

But how do we do this? We pray and ask for help. The Holy Spirit is ready and waiting to guide us and intercede for us in prayer; we simply need to ask (1 John 3:22 (KJV). We start small, and in fact you have begun just that with this book, this study. Begin thinking of changes you can make in your life as you continue reading and meeting in your groups. Next, formally list those changes in writing, and share them with someone as a form of accountability. Are you beginning to form that list? I know I am!

22And whatsoever we ask, we receive of him, because we keep his commandments, and do those things that are pleasing in his sight. I John 3:22 (KJV)

Bible Verses & Notes

Session 3
Discussion Points

1. Think about God's advice to not look on the outward appearance but as He does, upon someone's heart. What would you say this means in our everyday dealings with others?

2. What differences can you see between the biblical duties discussed and those listed for the royal family?

3. What are some traditions your family shares? They can be things such as attending seasonal gala events, tailgating, or holiday festivities. Do they help you focus on your heart or your outward appearance? Ouch— looking at gatherings through those eyes is now causing me to have heartburn, what about y'all?

4. Have you taken the step to formally list in writing those areas in your life where change can occur facilitating your relationship with Jesus? If so, please share them within your group or with a trusted friend.

THE DUTY WE HAVE TO OURSELVES: BEING TREATED AS A DAUGHTER OF THE KING

Bible Verses & Notes

Each word and every thought in this book and study has been an inspiration from God through the Holy Spirit's guidance. OK, maybe not the occasional, comical sidebars; those are just my way of lightening the mood and making you smile. I have been led to write based on my upbringing and teachings gleaned from all those vacation Bible schools, youth retreats, choir tours, and mission trips during my church life; my research through countless Bible studies and inspirational readings; and my life experiences. I should also mention my most favorite thing to do— watching people and their interactions with others. Yes, I am a person who does not mind eating alone or, because I get sick riding roller coasters, holding all the souvenirs purchased while others ride. I'm content sitting in the middle of the mall and watching people. Normally during the months known as fall by most but known in the South as football season, my husband and I, plus eighty-seven thousand others, are sitting in Jordan Hare Stadium in Auburn, Alabama, on any given Saturday. Auburn does not always play as well as I think they should, so I end up watching all those people on the sidelines and in the stands. I have learned many things just from that. Let us also add to this equation my love for reading, watching movies, and television shows. Remember, I grew up in a time when that was all one had for entertainment—no computers, no handheld devices, and no gaming devices. I can quote lines from movies and beloved TV shows because my brain holds such items for use when they may be needed.

Consequently, this session about our duty to ourselves— meaning how we, as daughters of the King, chosen by God, and loved by Jesus, are to be treated by others—is a major reason for writing this book and study.

First and foremost, I want you all to accept Jesus as your Lord and Savior. Begin that best friend forever relationship with Him so we can all spend eternity in heaven. Have hope here on Earth and foster love for our neighbors because of our love for Jesus. But beyond this, I want all young girls and adult women to understand how treasured we are in God's kingdom. During His ministry, Jesus elevated women to a place that was groundbreaking for that era. We need to remind ourselves and the world of this now because I sense we are allowing society to lower our standards of respect.

In the effort to become "equal with men," we have taken away our right to be treated as ladies and as women who follow the teachings of Christ. Please understand that I will be the first to grab a ladder and climb on the soap box to ensure equal pay for equal work. (You see, I am only five feet, almost two inches tall, depending on the humidity and my hair and I cannot jump on that soapbox any longer due to too many twelve-hour shifts and too many years of being overweight and climbing in and out of ambulances as a transport nurse).

I do have a passion for crime dramas, courtroom dramas, and the law, but I could not fathom sitting through a class on contracts or business law. Therefore, even with a Master of Science degree from a School of Law and many years of television viewing, I cannot technically try a case in a court of law. But I can present a passionate argument when necessary. These next thoughts are mine, and I do understand these folks of whom I speak do work hard to get where they are professionally, so back down, Momma Simba. But really, y'all, can we honestly say it is OK to pay someone millions, or up to billions, of dollars to perform an athletic function, and while these people are doing so, it is acceptable to make mistakes? I mean one continues to receive said amount regardless of the fumbles, dropped passes, wrong plays called due to reading a defense badly, poor tackling technique in open space, missing a kick, missing a free throw (do not get me started on this one), or dropping a pop fly to center field. Yet a teacher, fireman, policeman, nurse, and our military forces, who perform in life-and-death situations each day, must work overtime or extra shifts simply to live paycheck to paycheck.

We shall not even begin to travel down the road of what happens if those people make a mistake in their work functions. Let me just say if I miscalculated a drug dose and the decimal point was off by 0.1, not only could a life be lost and a family would suffer a tragedy, but my family would lose everything, and I would suffer as well. Many nurses commit suicide from innocent mistakes like that.

Bible Verses & Notes

21So the Lord God caused a deep sleep to come over the man, and he slept. God took one of his ribs and closed the flesh at that place. 22Then the Lord God made the rib He had taken from the man into a woman and brought her to the man. 23And the man said: This one, at last, is bone of my bone and flesh of my flesh; this one will be called "woman," for she was taken from man. 24This is why a man leaves his father and mother and bonds with his wife, and they become one flesh. Genesis 2:21-24

Bible Verses & Notes

I am sorry, but the equation of equal pay for equal work cannot be balanced in our society today. Using the argument for example just presented one may conclude neither male nor female wins in present day's culture when it comes to equality in the work force. Here you are catching a glimpse into my science geekiness. I am one who tries hard to make equations balance, as I was taught in math and chemistry. That's the way God made me and how my brain works. So why continue in this lose-lose situation the world has placed us in?

Let's take charge, accept the fact we cannot balance that equation without a major revolution, and stop beating our heads against that proverbial wall. I have enough headaches without adding more triggers to the list. How about you? What we can change is our expectations, our beliefs in how we want to be treated by others.

We have established the Bible as our safest and most reliable source as a reference and guide. Using the Bible, let us start at the beginning, Genesis 2:21–24, when God made the first woman out of a rib of man. Now we shall present another case. Because we were made from man, we are now considered a part of him: "bone of my bone," "flesh of my flesh" (Genesis 2: 23HCSB). The foundation for the marriage covenant is set in that the two are united as one flesh (Genesis 2: 24 HCSB).

Stop and ponder on this. Would any man talk to, hit, laugh at, curse at, demean with his language or his treatment of himself as he does his wife or any woman? Or would he even think of those actions or behaviors toward all manner of other men? I think not. First, if he did so to himself; society would label him a lunatic or as having mental health issues, and they would have him committed as a harm to himself or others. Second, if he did so to another male; he runs the risk of harm being inflicted upon him—you know getting the livin' daylights (I have yet to figure out exactly what those are) knocked out of him, as we say in the South. Either way, he is rightly to be considered one brick shy of a load!

Then we notice one of my memory verses, Proverbs 31:31*, where God is telling the man to reward this wife just described for all her efforts. From the King James Version to the Complete

Jewish Study Bible, this verse is saying she deserves a portion of the "fruit" or harvest obtained from the work she does. The sixties and seventies did not have to radicalize how women are to be treated. God had already given us the "Women's Bill of Rights" throughout the Bible. We, as disciples or students, simply need to raise our awareness of this knowledge and become bold enough to speak out as instructed in Psalm 68:11* (New International Version). Let this become our battle cry, ladies: We are a mighty throng! Now, we must be careful and include all lettering in the word *throng*, or otherwise ouch! Enough said on that one.

As we move into the New Testament, in Ephesians 5:23–33 and 1 Timothy 3:1–13, we see God's handbook for "God like households" and "God like men." Men are to treat us as Christ treats His church, His body. Therefore, let us see what happened when Jesus felt His church was not being treated properly during the latter part of His ministry, as He had just entered the city of Jerusalem after being heralded as blessed. The crowds shouted and announced Him as The King, the one coming in the name of the Lord! He finds the outer gates of the temple (the church vestibule) being used to sell secondhand animals for sacrifice. I really enjoy reading the recording of this in John 2:13–17. Here, I see our Savior bustin' a rod, as we say in the South. He made a whip out of cords and overturned those tables in a manner that coins were scattered while he threw out the men sitting at those tables. In other words, Jesus cleaned house!

Do you not agree that as women, we need to clean house, in a manner of speaking? We should clean out the idea we are to settle for whatever that significant other's ill-mannered actions toward us might be. We should clean out the idea that we are to be treated any way other than how one wants to be treated themselves.

Now, I am not naïve enough to think those in abusive situations can simply walk out right now. Having worked with as many females as I have over the past thirty-plus years, I have encountered such circumstances either as a coworker or as a caregiver to an infant's mother. It takes a huge amount of prayer, courage, and faith to reach out, admit the circumstance exists, and ask for help. Then it takes planning, especially if children are involved. But the

Bible Verses & Notes

12This is My command: Love one another as I have loved you. John 15:12

32And be kind and compassionate to one another, forgiving one another, just as God also forgave you in Christ. Ephesians 4:32

Bible Verses & Notes

situation must be handled in some way for all those involved before serious harm or death occurs.

Our case concludes that men should treat women as Jesus treated women, as the Bible teaches, we should be treated, and as we deserve to be treated. We are a part of them and a reflection of the body of Jesus, His church. God also wants us to remember what is written about loving one another in general.

Once we love God and love Jesus, who loved us so much He gave up everything, even His life for us, then we can begin to love others, forgive others, and more important love and forgive ourselves (John 15:12; Ephesians 4:32).

So, ladies of the kingdom, are we willing to allow men or society to defile our heavenly Father, our Abba, or our Savior Jesus with their language—much less to defile or demean us with their language, with their media, and or with their actions and behavior? As King David so eloquently stated in Psalm 68:11*(NIV), we women who proclaim the Word of God are a mighty throng! We shall embrace that thought so we can become just that.

Young women, I ask you to take a stand and begin laying your foundation. Mothers and more "seasoned" women, we too are to pray ahead for our young ladies, asking God to guide them to that one godly man He has chosen for them. We should ask Him to help them not settle and remind them of their place as His children. We must ask Him to help us earn respect and expect respect. We need to have such feelings of worthiness and honor as daughters of the King that when someone speaks or acts in a manner disrespectful to God or to us, we lovingly raise their awareness to our standards of care, to our ethical and moral code of conduct. If you were to write an ethical code of conduct for yourself, what would be included? That is another thing to ponder on the porch.

When we begin to lovingly—you see, I need to remind myself of that word, *lovingly*—speak out for our God and ourselves, we may lose some friends. Were they really friends? Or were they like those at the tables selling secondhand goods, and they need to be driven out? We are His house, His church, a house of prayer!

Well now, ladies, we must do our part to ensure this newfound respect is maintained, meaning we must present ourselves in a way the world will say is different. It will set the stage for our expectations and how others think of us. God obviously feels women are of utmost importance and therefore should be treated as such. We need only think about a few of the many instances God demonstrates the love He has for women and the power of His women:

- After four hundred years of silence, who was one of the first to hear from the Holy Spirit? Mary, the soon to be mother of Jesus. Think about this. God is God. He did not really need Mary, did He? He could have simply placed Jesus on Earth in human form as an adult. But He wanted Him born of a woman, a virgin. That is the least likely way to show His power and for us to give Him glory.
- Whom was the first person our resurrected Savior, Jesus, spoke to? Mary Magdalene—not any of His men known as disciples, but a woman with a past.
- Who risked her life and saved the Jewish nation? Queen Esther. If you ever need a wonderful pick-me-up read, please do so with the book of Esther. She is one of my role models "for such a time as this" (Esther 4:14 HCSB).

It is safe to say that as females, we have allowed an injustice to be placed upon ourselves by the world, society, and the evil one. We need only consider this observation made a few years ago when attempting to find suitable television viewing for my boys. How did we, as a church body, much less women of God, move from the husband-and-wife duo Lucy and Ricky Ricardo on *I Love Lucy*[14] sleeping in separate beds to females parading on a runway as angels in their skimpy undergarments, leaving nothing to the imagination? Being seen during primetime viewing hours. Herein lies the basis of many issues regarding the treatment of women today.

Bible Verses & Notes

14If you keep silent at this time, liberation and deliverance will come to the Jewish people from another place, but you and your father's house will be destroyed. Who knows, perhaps you have come to your royal position for such a time as this." Esther 4:14

HOW DO OTHERS REACT TO THE BRITISH ROYAL FAMILY?

As we move to our comparative look into the royal family and their expectations regarding interactions with others; think on this. As a royal, people open doors for you. As a daughter of the King, God opens the door for you. Wow, that is deep. This is a glimpse of the Holy Spirit and my brain at work while researching information and watching episodes of *The Crown* for the third or fourth time.

Of course, royals are to be approached and thought of in a manner of utmost respect. The difference is this type of respect is based on tradition and a title. It has not necessarily been earned by the deeds or actions of that person. Members of the royal family receive a bow, a curtsey, or an address denoting their title simply due to their birth or whom they marry.

The ruling king or queen is the top of the hierarchy. The person literally leads the line, meaning everyone walks a certain distance behind him or her, including a spouse or former heads of state. Keep in mind all others are part of the group of subjects over which they rule. This order of who's who includes a specific seating order at meals, special events, and even family functions. If more than one member of the royal family is present in a room, there is an order as to the first acknowledged, the second, and so on.

This respect begins even before birth because traditionally, the gender of the royal infant is not disclosed prior to birth. So, no bonfire gender-reveal barbeque hoedowns at Buckingham palace, I suppose. Another tidbit I found in my research is if you were to draw Queen Elizabeth's name for Christmas, do not get a Monopoly game. Rumor has it this game is forbidden among the family. Do you think maybe they have some feuding going on as well? Let us not forget about the queen's famous purse, signaling for conversations to end as well as meals that are completed.[15]

As we can surmise, being a monarch or a member of this family commands a type of respect. Again, it does not mean you are well liked, well thought of, or loved for being you. It is a result of your name, your title, your spouse, and your lineage. We have seen in our lifetime that one can have instances of poor decision-making that can cause one to no longer be considered a member of this family.

As we think of God's kingdom and being a child in it, how do our poorly made decisions affect our standing in this kingdom? Are you sitting on the porch swing pondering this one? Once we become daughters of the King, not only are we heirs while on Earth, but we are also His children for eternity. The respect we earn through our love for others, our faith-filled works, and our Christlike attitude found through the fruits of the Spirit (Galatians 5:22-23) is everlasting and felt to be genuine by others. Even though the world or society sees us as different, in the end they too will want what we have.

To complete this session, I would like for everyone to apply the concept of respect as a daughter of the King, to her life and current circumstances. Readers may find it helpful to write out scenarios for question 1 and then answer question 2 for self-reflection.

For group participants, have some scenarios ready, either from personal experiences or from potential experiences, to use for question 1, and have thoughts on question 2 for class discussion as you feel comfortable to share.

Bible Verses & Notes

Session 4
Discussion Points

1. How would you handle situations regarding inappropriate media, language, dating conditions, and marriage situations as a child of God?

2. What do you think are appropriate ways to present yourself as a child of God?

For the Comparison Chart

1. What did you see as differences, if any, between treatment as a child of God and treatment in the royal family?

THE PRICE OF ROYALTY

Bible Verses & Notes

I cannot believe we have almost completed our journey to becoming conformed, glorified, faith filled women ready to collectively take on our personal demons and the evil one as daughters of the Most High King. We are not alone in this fight, because we have the Holy Spirit to guide us and intercede for us when we pray (Romans 8:26–27), and now we have each other. Remember Psalm 68:11*, as translated **in** the New International Version, which states we are learning the Word, ready to announce it and proclaim it in faith as the Truth, so we are a mighty throng!

But let us not forget a couple of our responsibilities.

- By putting Jesus first, others second, and yourself last, you have spelled out JOY. Receive joy while taking up whatever is your cross at that time and following where Jesus leads (Luke 9:23*).
- Keep the most important commandments according to Jesus (Mark 12:28–31). When asked this by a religious leader trying to discredit him during His ministry, Jesus simply stated those ideals learned as a young Jewish boy, which we find in Deuteronomy 6:4–6. We are to understand our Lord is the one and only God. We are to love Him with everything we have capable of loving, meaning our hearts, souls, minds, and strength. With this love of God, we are to then love others—and He meant all others—as ourselves. Can you imagine what our world would be like if those two simple concepts were obeyed, even by just those who claim to be followers of Christ? That is food for thought as we round the corner on this lap of our journey.

The world looks at these duties or responsibilities and says we are sacrificing things for our faith. I have personally been told this by family members and acquaintances. OK, so what things? Friends who now feel uncomfortable around us because we ask them to not speak unkindly about our Lord when they use His name in anger. Or friends that say we cramp their style because we prefer not to (1) continue treating our bodies as anything other than the temple God created and (2) waste money on substances that alter our thought processes and cause us to lose control of situations. These are friends whom we now are trying to help become better people because that is what a true friend does. Therefore, were these people really our friends or just folks using us to help boost their self-esteem while they search for that quick-fix substance to fill their God-sized space? Do you see why I use the word *acquaintances* now instead of *friends* when speaking with others about this topic?

Some may say we sacrifice fun. As far as I can tell, this notion is based on one's definition of fun. If fun is attempting to fill your God-sized space with substances that cause you to eventually lose control of your actions and behaviors in a manner leading to harm of others or yourself, then as far as this equation, subtract that substrate because I am fine with sacrificing it! What about you? I would rather remember those outings with friends spent laughing at myself and each other's shortcomings and goofy antics done in the attempt to be "too cool for school." Come on, ladies; you know from whence I speak. Those expensive, body-harming substances cause one to pass out, and then those "fun times" are forgotten.

The Bible tells us in Matthew 19:29 that if we are to forsake anything for our faith, such as those who must leave the religion of their family and consequently are lost to that family, or those who must leave their homeland, then we will receive blessings one hundred times more and inherit eternal life. Let me pause for a second before someone decides I have become a television evangelist saying, "Give up all your money and your house and send it to me so you can then receive one hundred times more in return!" Correct me if I am wrong, but I do not think that is how it was meant in that passage. What Jesus—and yes, as we can see in the HCSB, like many other translations, the words of Jesus are emphasized by using red lettering —was telling us is this: Those who have given up things, even their families, to follow Him will receive their greatest reward when He returns to Earth and occupies His glorious throne. They will sit on thrones with Him and spend eternity with Him in heaven. And that, my friend, is worth one hundred times more. Now, am I saying we do not

Bible Verses & Notes

29And everyone who has left houses, brothers or sisters, father or mother, children, or fields because of My name will receive 100 times more and will inherit eternal life. Matthew 19:29

Bible Verses & Notes

28We know that all things work together for the good of those who love God: those who are called according to His purpose. Romans 8:28

28When Jesus had finished this sermon, the crowds were astonished at His teaching, 29because He was teaching them like one who had authority, and not like their scribes. Matthew 7:28-29

12In fact, all those who want to live a godly life in Christ Jesus will be persecuted. II Timothy 3:12

10Now the God of all grace, who called you to His eternal glory in Christ Jesus, will personally restore, establish, strengthen, and support you after you have suffered a little. I Peter 5:10

11For I know the plans I have for you" — this is the Lord's declaration — "plans for your welfare, not for disaster, to give you a future and a hope. Jeremiah 29:11

receive blessings here and now? Of course not. But some days that "fog of life" can get pretty thick, and we will have to squint and look closely through it to find them. Believe me, they are there. It may be that at your doctor's appointment, they say you have a credit on your account, and your copay is way less than you anticipated. Or you hit End on your phone, after talking with a bill collector who is half your age and trying to give you advice while flipping through a "go to" chart and see the most gorgeous sunset painted on the sky, just for you. There to remind you God is with you and in control. Yes, those are real happenings in my life, and yes, I teared up again while writing about them. I am really not as tough as I seem.

Romans 8 details the life of a follower of Christ. It reminds us of what life without Jesus was like and then paints a beautiful picture of our new life with Him. It reminds us we now have the Spirit of God and are His children. We can now call God, Abba, our Daddy! As children, we are heirs of God and coheirs with Christ. This means we share in His suffering so we can also share in His glory. Also, within this chapter is another of my favorite memory verses, Romans 8:28. If I had a nickel for each time this verse brought me out of a storm, that bill collector would have stopped calling a long time back!

During His ministry, Jesus experienced the same reactions from others as we have experienced or will experience in our current times. When people heard His name, Jesus of Nazareth, they commented, "Can anything good come from that town? What does that guy know? He is from the other side of the tracks," as we would say here in the South (John 1:45–46). The religious leaders felt His teachings imposed upon their financial and community status, so they would undermine and question Him while He talked with the crowds. Sound familiar? It went to the extent that they would point out His earthly parents and interrogate Him, saying, "You say you are the Son of God, but I thought Joseph of Nazareth and Mary were you mother and father. How can you be both the Messiah, a Son of God, and their son as well?" I am paraphrasing John 6:41–42 with some down-home terms. But, as Matthew 7:28–29 tells us, the people believed Him and were amazed because He spoke to them and taught them as one with knowledge, as one of them, not as the religious leaders spoke to and taught them.

God knew we would suffer as followers of His Son. He even tells us we will in 2 Timothy 3:12. But God provides help (1 Peter 5:10), letting us know the suffering is for a short time, and afterward He will restore us and make us stronger, firmer, and ready for a new journey He has planned (Jeremiah 29:11; another memory verse). You see, Jesus knew God's plan for Him. Let us sit on the porch and swing a minute on this one. Pretend you know you were born to bear the sins of all the current world's population and those of future generations. You know you would be accused of crimes not committed, found guilty, and sentenced to die by the hands of Roman soldiers, who are expert killers. Jesus literally sweated blood while praying the night before His death, asking God, "Take this cup," but He ended His prayer with, "Not my will but Yours, be done" (Luke 22:41–44 HCSB). Therefore, it is OK to ask God questions when we pray and get that frustration off our chest. However, just as Jesus did, we do need to remind ourselves that God's will, not ours, is best.

As we see, one of the hardest things about being children of God is doing battle with the evil one as he attempts to discredit our faith and our testimony. What do I mean by this?

The evil one needs the world to see followers of Jesus as weak, hypocritical, and doubtful of our trust and faith in the gospel and the Bible. As we discussed in Session One, God outlines a battle plan for us in Ephesians 6:10-18*. He gives us our daily attire of armor which we can assemble to resist and help defeat the evil one. Having my life rope, with its memory verse knots, helps me as I go into battle and as I help others prepare for their battles. What additional defenses have you found useful in your daily battles? Jot them down for use in your small group or as references when a friend is facing a battle of their own.

Even if the world says you have sacrificed things to become a follower of Jesus, can you honestly say those things made you a better person? The person God intended you to be. The person Jesus died for. Who is really looking out for us, the world or our

3The Lord appeared to us in the past, saying: "I have loved you with an everlasting love; I have drawn you with unfailing kindness. Jeremiah 31:3 (NIV)

17You will be hated by everyone because of My name. Luke 21:17

1But know this: Difficult times will come in the last days. II Timothy 3:1

8But you will receive power when the Holy Spirit has come on you, and you will be My witnesses in Jerusalem, in all Judea and Samaria, and to the ends of the earth." Acts 1:8

heavenly Father? Our Abba, who sent Jesus as the ultimate sacrifice for us. The Father, who promises to love us "with an everlasting love and unfailing kindness" (Jeremiah 31:3 NIV). I know the answers to these questions, and I am ready to boldly defend them. What are your answers, and can you defend them? My prayer is that if you cannot feel comfortable saying yes loudly, you are at least thinking about your answers and talking with someone you have found to be a trusted, godly mentor.

If this is the case, then I know the will of God has been and will continue to be at work in our life! For a daughter of the King, any sacrifice is for the gospel.

WHAT DOES A ROYAL SOVEREIGN SURRENDER FOR THEIR CROWN?

As for the sacrifices one sees within the role of a monarch, once again we are talking about their obligations to the Crown—those responsibilities overshadowing their callings as a wife, mother, or a person in general. The way I see it, the sovereign of a country sacrifices wants and needs for the sake of the Crown. Society, and the world as a whole, sees that crown as material gains, stardom, and living in a palace—being able to buy what you want whenever you want it, as long as it fits the dress code or standards of the Crown.

I am quite sure some monarchs—Queen Victoria and her husband, Albert, as an example—did marry for love, but many have been forced to marry for the Crown or monarchy? As for one's calling, maybe one might want to work as a large animal doctor. Growing up with access to many horses fostered a love for them, correct? Then there are those hats, I get a migraine just thinking about wearing some of them all day. Of course, the whole etiquette and protocol thing would surely do me in. I know I would mess that up worse than some of our presidents. The thing I would get right is the "Yes, ma'am" and "No, ma'am" and the "Bless her heart" thing, provided that is their thing!

On a more serious note, I dare say the current royal family, and everyone in a way, felt the pangs of loss due to fame and stardom associated to being a royal. But as any who are followers of Jesus know,

God is in control, and He has a master plan for each of us. When we are reading chapter 5 of our book, He has already completed the book!

The bottom line is something might only be considered a true sacrifice if it was given up out of unconditional love and if its loss makes a change for the better. With this in mind, have you or I, living in America, really sacrificed anything of importance to become a follower of Jesus? I think about and pray for our fellow believers living with families or in areas in which confessing a faith outside of the family's religious background or the government's preference can lead to abandonment and death (Mark 13: 9–13). There are some like this in America today, and we should all pray for them and their struggles, asking God to provide them strength, courage, and protection. Most Americans have probably felt discomfort and maybe embarrassment when unable to defend their faith; lately, they may have experienced loss of work as they attempt to defend their faith (Luke 21:17).

These are the storm clouds gathering on the horizon that Jesus foretold of when asked about His return (Luke 21:25–28). Our churches establish safety plans that include active shooter drills and policies. This makes me understand that our persecution is increasing, and the level of it will continue to increase until He returns on those clouds. Woe to those who remain to experience the reign of the antichrist once God has finally determined the time has come (Mark 13:19–23; 2 Timothy 3:1).

It is for this reason God has given me a new calling, a new journey. Yes, I am now a woman on a mission to strengthen other women so we may become that mighty throng found in Psalm 68:11* (NIV). In this way, we can then follow the last command of Jesus: go out and teach everyone about Him, His love, and how they can become children of God (Matthew 28:19-20*; Mark 16:15-16; Acts 1:8) so we can prepare His way!

To begin your mission and for me to continue my mission, we must now make our game plan, our battle plan. Reading and working through this book, this group study, is a huge first step. For now, I pray you can all say boldly, proudly, and loudly, "I am a daughter of the Most High King." Understand your acceptance of Jesus as your Savior, as the coheir who shed His blood to cover

Bible Verses & Notes

your sins and give you access to the heavenly Father. Be ready to take on the roles and assignments we discussed. Declare, "I am to be respected. I will present myself as a woman of God and as such do not tolerate behavior, language, and actions that the Bible teaches are unacceptable."

Again, if questions remain unanswered, or if you have not found someone nearby to talk or pray with about a faith-filled acceptance of Jesus, I press upon you the urgency of this need. Time is of the essence, as I have yet to find the birth certificate form that includes an expiration date. That's gruesome I realize, but it's a fact, nonetheless. We have no assurance of tomorrow.

Once the mighty throng is in place, our game plan should start within our homes, our local churches, and our communities. If A helps B, then B helps C who then helps D, and so forth, that means A has helped many people. That may not make sense in your mind, but in the world according to me, it makes perfect sense.

The point is this: For me, once I analyzed the Great Commission, or the words spoken by Jesus telling us one of our most important duties, I discovered it contains verbs and action words: *go*, *teach*, *baptize*, and *immerse*. The Complete Jewish Bible uses the Hebrew word *Tevilah*, or full-body immersion. In the Old Testament, the children of Israel would perform a water baptism or immersion in a body of water—a Tevilah—in order to cleanse themselves before approaching God. The act of doing this cleansing is termed the mikveh, which means cleansing.[16] John was a cousin of Jesus, and his mother, Elizabeth, was one of the first people Mary went to see after being told by the angel Gabriel that she would give birth to Jesus. Later he would be known as John the Baptizer (John 1:29–39). He was the first of his kind in many ways. He became the original preparer of the Way, and he led in announcing the first appearance of Jesus as the Messiah. He began immersing the Jewish community as a sign of repentance, helping them emerge as new people.

We are to follow John's example, helping others with their salvation journey while we prepare for the Way, for the second and most glorious appearance of Jesus, when that trumpet sounds and time shall be no more (1 Thessalonians 4:16–18).

Session 5
Discussion Points

These final questions for readers and for groups to use in their concluding session will allow us to bring the game plan home and make it personal.

1. What actions can you take alone to prepare for the Way, for the second coming of Jesus?

2. What are some ideas for your group, a small group at a church, or any group of daughters willing to help in your area?

3. What will be your first step?

4. What will be the first step of your group?

Please share all answers, as you are willing within your group or with a trusted faith-filled friend. Because, as we have discussed, a rope is stronger with more strands and knots added to it.

Bible Verses & Notes

13and in the middle of the lampstands I saw one like a son of man, clothed in a robe reaching to the feet, and wrapped around the chest with a golden sash. 14His head and His hair were white like white wool, like snow; and His eyes were like a flame of fire. 15His feet were like burnished bronze when it has been heated to a glow in a furnace, and His voice was like the sound of many waters. 16In His right hand He held seven stars, and out of His mouth came a sharp two-edged sword; and His face was like the sun shining in its strength.

17When I saw Him, I fell at His feet like a dead man. And He placed His right hand on me, saying, "Do not be afraid; I am the first and the last, 18and the living One; and I was dead, and behold, I am alive forevermore, and I have the keys of death and of Hades.

Revelation 1:13-18 (New American Standard Bible 2020)

Bible Verses & Notes

For the Comparison Chart:

1. What do you see as sacrifices being made by followers of Christ today? In America? In other countries? Focus specifically on sacrifices made by women of God.

2. What sacrifices are made by a ruling British sovereign? Do you see any difference between those made by a queen or by a king?

3. Whose sacrifice is more costly, more worthy, and more everlasting—those of a sovereign, or those of a woman following Christ?

It is my hope and prayer that each reader finds a way to print their own Certificate of Adoption & Completion as well as obtain a charm which can denote their Crown of Faith. I feel these items will serve as visual representations of your commitment as a daughter of the King and as a member of the mighty throng. They can serve to open doors as you begin to prepare the Way. Meaning the second appearance of Jesus on Earth. This time He will appear not as a baby but as the Mighty King described by the Apostle John in Revelation 1:13–18.

COMPARISON CHART FORMAT

This is a suggested format for a Comparison Chart. It is the one I designed for my first class participating in this Bible study. I found it helpful to allow space for writing styles and each learner's input.

COMPARISON CHART		
SESSION # & DATES	GOD'S KINGDOM	BRITISH ROYAL FAMILY
ONE	STEPS:	STEPS:
TWO	CORONATION CEREMONY:	CORONATION CEREMONY:

THREE	DUTIES:	DUTIES:
FOUR	TREATMENT AS CHILD OF GOD:	TREATMENT AS A ROYAL MONARCH:
FIVE	SACRIFICES:	SACRIFICES OF QUEEN VS KING:

CERTIFICATE OF ADOPTION & ACHIEVEMENT FORMAT

This is a suggested format for a group's Certificate of Adoption and Achievement referenced within the book.

CERTIFICATE OF ADOPTION AND ACHIEVEMENT

This acknowledges that upon this day, in the year designated and by the biblical standards set forth in Romans 8:15-17 and Galatians 3:26-29, the following disciple has become an adopted child of God, having presented herself and recognized as a daughter of the King.

NAME

By confessing herself a sinner, accepting Christ as her Savior, and asking Him to occupy the throne of her heart in a prayer of repentance, she now accepts all rights, privileges, honors, and responsibilities as authorized through scripture to become a daughter of the King.

DATE
MONTH, DAY, YEAR

PASTOR OR GROUP
LEADER

HELPFUL HINTS

For those using this book as a group Bible study I am passing along these items, as suggestions, based on evaluations of classes taught this material.

- Classes have discussed the importance of conveying to new followers of Christ, and honestly to some of us even more seasoned followers as well, the idea of our relationship with Christ as a covenant. With this in mind, we have found the coronation ceremony of a British sovereign, with its 5 stages, to be a very moving and reflective imagery of this same covenant. Therefore, we incorporate those same stages in our ceremony:
   - Recognition- in which the participants are presented as followers and the group verbally recognizes them.
   - Oath- that part in which they verbally profess to make this lifelong promise in the presence of God and others.
   - Anointing- the time for use of oil to promote service of hands, indicate their heart as the throne of God, and their mind being transformed.
   - Crowning- here is where they receive an actual crown as part of their armor of God, to use as a symbol of this covenant along with their helmet of salvation, and to be placed at the feet of Jesus once they arrive in Heaven. Many of those in my classes use their crowns to lift their spirits on those fog-filled days we all have.
   - Homage- we use this as a time of prayer over our ladies to honor their commitment and to ask for God's protection over them.
- Crowns and robes for each participant during the coronation ceremony. Either attend that church business meeting, you know the one of which I speak, in which budgets are discussed and include these as line items, or have your church sewing

group begin working on those robes. Also, I found this session could become a time of fun and fellowship by allowing two weeks for its completion and serving special "coronation foods", such as scones, cucumber sandwiches, and punch. I even brought out the Lennox fine dinnerware out of the cabinet for my classes. We really try to make this a special day with pictures and special music.

- An essential oil or some type of fragrant oil and a serving spoon or ladle to use for the anointing part of the coronation ceremony. Please keep in mind those, like me, who may have certain scents as migraine triggers when choosing your oil.

- Another detail for Session Two is some means in which your class may view Queen Elizabeth II's coronation. Either a documentary version or an episode within a series.

- I also bring a rope to class to illustrate my Life Rope and its knots mentioned in Session Three.

- As Session Three and Four contain some deep and thought-provoking discussion topics we have found these may need two weeks as well for due diligence to be given and time management.

- Each participant in my classes receives a charm, a Crown of Faith I call it, at the end of the study. I just order them or try and find them on sale at local craft stores. Again, an item for you to think about in your budget.

I hope you find these enhance your classes and make them a fun experience for all those attending. Each time I teach a class this material I too receive many blessings and learn something new.

ADDITIONAL REFERENCED
SCRIPTURE PASSAGES

1On the first day of the week Mary Magdalene came to the tomb early, while it was still dark. She saw that the stone had been removed from the tomb. 2So she ran to Simon Peter and to the other disciple, the one Jesus loved, and said to them, "They have taken the Lord out of the tomb, and we don't know where they have put Him!" 3At that, Peter and the other disciple went out, heading for the tomb. 4The two were running together, but the other disciple outran Peter and got to the tomb first. 5Stooping down, he saw the linen cloths lying there, yet he did not go in. 6Then, following him, Simon Peter came also. He entered the tomb and saw the linen cloths lying there, yet he did not go in. 6Then, following him, Simon Peter came also. He entered the tomb and saw the linen cloths lying there. 7The wrapping that had been on His head was not lying with the linen cloths but was folded up in a separate place by itself. 8The other disciple, who had reached the tomb first, then entered the tomb, saw, and believed. 9For they still did not understand the Scripture that He must rise from the dead. 10Then the disciples went home again. 11But Mary stood outside facing the tomb, crying. As she was crying, she stooped to look into the tomb. 12She saw two angels in white sitting there, one at the head and one at the feet, where Jesus' body had been lying. 13They said to her, "Woman, why are you crying?" "Because they've taken away my Lord," she told them, "and I don't know where they've put Him." 14Having said this, she turned around and saw Jesus standing there, though she did not know it was Jesus. 15"Woman," Jesus said to her, "why are you crying? Who is it you are looking for?" Supposing He was the gardener, she replied, "Sir, if you've removed Him, tell me where you've put Him, and I will take Him away." 16Jesus said, "Mary." Turning around, she said to Him in Hebrew, *"Rabbouni!"* — which means "Teacher." John 20:1-16

10Who can find a capable wife? She is far more precious than jewels. 11The heart of her husband trusts in her, and he will not lack anything good. 12She rewards him with good, not evil, all the days of her life. 13She selects wool and flax and works with willing hands. 14She is like the merchant ships, bringing her food from far away. 15She rises while it is still night and provides food for her household and portions for her female servants. 16She evaluates a field and buys it; she plants a vineyard with her earnings. 17She draws on her strength and reveals that her arms are strong. 18She sees that her profits are good, and her lamp never goes out at night. 19She extends her hands to the spinning staff, and her hands hold the spindle. 20Her hands reach out to the poor, and she extends her hands to the needy. 21She is not afraid for her household when it snows,

for all in her household are doubly clothed. 22She makes her own bed coverings; her clothing is fine linen and purple. 23Her husband is known at the city gates, where he sits among the elders of the land. 24She makes and sells linen garments; she delivers belts to the merchants. 25Strength and honor are her clothing, and she can laugh at the time to come. 26She opens her mouth with wisdom and loving instruction is on her tongue. 27She watches over the activities of her household and is never idle. 28Her sons rise up and call her blessed. Her husband also praises her: 29"Many women are capable, but you surpass them all!" 30Charm is deceptive and beauty is fleeting, but a woman who fears the Lord will be praised.

*31Give her the reward of her labor, and let her works praise her at the city gates. Proverbs 31:10-31

7Then the Lord said, "I have observed the misery of My people in Egypt, and have heard them crying out because of their oppressors, and I know about their sufferings. 8I have come down to rescue them from the power of the Egyptians and to bring them from that land to a good and spacious land, a land flowing with milk and honey — the territory of the Canaanites, Hittites, Amorites, Perizzites, Hivites, and Jebusites. 9The Israelites' cry for help has come to Me, and I have also seen the way the Egyptians are oppressing them. 10Therefore, go. I am sending you to Pharaoh so that you may lead My people, the Israelites, out of Egypt." Exodus 3:7-10

23for the husband is the head of the wife as Christ is the head of the church. He is the Savior of the body. 24Now as the church submits to Christ, so wives are to submit to their husbands in everything. 25Husbands, love your wives, just as Christ loved the church and gave Himself for her 26to make her holy, cleansing her with the washing of water by the word. 27He did this to present the church to Himself in splendor, without spot or wrinkle or anything like that, but holy and blameless. 28In the same way, husbands are to love their wives as their own bodies. He who loves his wife loves himself. 29For no one ever hates his own flesh but provides and cares for it, just as Christ does for the church, 30since we are members of His body. 31For this reason a man will leave his father and mother and be joined to his wife, and the two will become one flesh. 32This mystery is profound, but I am talking about Christ and the church. 33To sum up, each one of you is to love his wife as himself, and the wife is to respect her husband. Ephesians 5:23-33

1This saying is trustworthy: "If anyone aspires to be an overseer, he desires a noble work." 2An overseer, therefore, must be above reproach, the husband of one wife, self-controlled, sensible, respectable, hospitable, an able teacher, 3not addicted to wine, not a bully but gentle, not quarrelsome, not greedy —4one who manages his own household competently, having his children under control with all dignity. 5(If anyone does not know how to manage his own household, how will he take care of God's church?) 6He must not be a new convert, or he might become conceited and fall into the condemnation of the Devil. 7Furthermore, he must have a good reputation among outsiders, so that he does not fall into disgrace and the Devil's trap. 8Deacons, likewise, should be worthy of respect, not hypocritical, not drinking a lot of wine, not greedy for money, 9holding the mystery of the faith with a clear conscience. 10And they must also be tested first; if they prove blameless, then they can serve as deacons. 11Wives, too, must be worthy of respect, not slanderers, self-controlled, faithful in everything. 12Deacons must be husbands of one wife, managing their children and their own households competently. 13For those who have served well as deacons acquire a good standing for themselves, and great boldness in the faith that is in Christ Jesus. I Timothy 3:1-13

4"Listen, Israel: The Lord our God, the Lord is One. 5Love the Lord your God with all your heart, with all your soul, and with all your strength. 6These words that I am giving you today are to be in your heart. Deuteronomy 6:4-6

45Philip found Nathanael and told him, "We have found the One Moses wrote about in the Law (and so did the prophets): Jesus the son of Joseph, from Nazareth!" 46"Can anything good come out of Nazareth?" Nathanael asked him. "Come and see," Philip answered. John 1:45-46

41Therefore the Jews started complaining about Him because He said, "I am the bread that came down from heaven." 42They were saying, "Isn't this Jesus the son of Joseph, whose father and mother we know? How can He now say, 'I have come down from heaven'?" John 6:41-42

41Then He withdrew from them about a stone's throw, knelt down, and began to pray, 42"Father, if You are willing, take this cup away from Me — nevertheless, not My will, but Yours, be done." 43Then an angel from heaven appeared to Him, strengthening Him. 44Being in anguish, He prayed more fervently, and His sweat became like drops of blood falling to the ground. Luke 22:41-44

9"But you, be on your guard! They will hand you over to sanhedrins, and you will be flogged in the synagogues. You will stand before governors and kings because of Me, as a witness to them. 10And the good news must first be proclaimed to all nations. 11So when they arrest you and hand you over, don't worry beforehand what you will say. On the contrary, whatever is given to you in that hour — say it. For it isn't you speaking, but the Holy Spirit. 12Then brother will betray brother to death, and a father his child. Children will rise up against parents and put them to death. 13And you will be hated by everyone because of My name. But the one who endures to the end will be delivered. Mark 13:9-13

25"Then there will be signs in the sun, moon, and stars; and there will be anguish on the earth among nations bewildered by the roaring sea and waves. 26People will faint from fear and expectation of the things that are coming on the world, because the celestial powers will be shaken. 27Then they will see the Son of Man coming in a cloud with power and great glory. 28But when these things begin to take place, stand up and lift up your heads, because your redemption is near!" Luke 21:25-28

19For those will be days of tribulation, the kind that hasn't been from the beginning of the world, which God created, until now and never will be again! 20Unless the Lord limited those days, no one would survive. But He limited those days because of the elect, whom He chose. 21"Then if anyone tells you, 'Look, here is the Messiah! Look — there!' do not believe it! 22For false messiahs and false prophets will rise up and will perform signs and wonders to lead astray, if possible, the elect. 23And you must watch! I have told you everything in advance. Mark 13:19-23

29The next day John saw Jesus coming toward him and said, "Here is the Lamb of God, who takes away the sin of the world! 30This is the One I told you about: 'After me comes a man who has surpassed me, because He existed before me.' 31I didn't know Him, but I came baptizing with water so He might be revealed to Israel." 32And John testified, "I watched the Spirit descending from heaven like a dove, and He rested on Him. 33I didn't know Him, but He who sent me to baptize with water told me, 'The One you see the Spirit descending and resting on — He is the One who baptizes with the Holy Spirit.' 34I have seen and testified that He is the Son of God!" 35Again the next day, John was standing with two of his disciples. 36When he saw Jesus passing by, he said, "Look! The Lamb of God!" 37The two disciples heard him say this and followed Jesus. 38When Jesus turned and noticed them following Him, He asked them, "What are you looking for?" They said to Him, "Rabbi" (which means "Teacher"), "where are You staying?" 39"Come and you'll see," He replied. John 1:29-39a

AFTERWORD

Dear daughters and fellow sisters of the kingdom,

I just wanted to drop a line or two and say how honored I am that (1) God led you to choose this book to read, or that He led you to attend the Bible study using this book as its guide; (2) you completed it, waded through the faith-inspired words and thoughts God placed in my brain, and tolerated all my feeble attempts at literary satire; and most importantly (3) you have accepted Jesus as your Savior and, like myself, are now an adopted child of God.

I cannot express the joy in my heart knowing all of you are my sistas, as we say in the South. My parents were older when I was born: my father was in his early forties, and my mother her late thirties. Remember me telling you he was a long-haul truck driver? Yes, I was a pleasant surprise, as my mother would always tell me. The closest sibling in age, my youngest brother, was nine years older than me. My sister was sixteen and my older brother was twelve when I was born. While growing up, I was basically an only child, because my siblings were married or serving in the military. Needless to say, I had many pretend friends until I started school, and to be honest, I kept some of those pretend friends even after then.

Knowing I now have the entire kingdom of God, including Jesus and all of you as coheirs and as my brothers and sisters makes me feel proud, loved, and never alone.

Even when, in the span of about five years, I experienced the death of my sister, my father, and my mother, I knew there are no orphans in God's kingdom! Grab a cup of coffee, hot chocolate, or a glass of sweet tea and sit on the porch swing for a minute on that one. How about that for comfort when the world has let you down?

God is now my heavenly Father, my Abba, and yours as well. He loves us, protects us, provides for us, and plans for us. But He also disciplines us when we are acting like the mischievous children we sometimes can be. I do think that heart of God we talked about probably breaks, as did mine when that wooden spoon had to be used on my boys. Because of His incomprehensible compassion, you know the compassion that sent Jesus for us, His heart breaks even more.

Now, just like any other group of sistas, we will disagree on items, and you know what? That is OK! For with the love of Christ in our hearts, we will always circle our wagons to protect each other and the gospel, because we are daughters of the King.

Let us go forward as the mighty throng, walking in the "paths of righteousness" (Psalm 23:3 KJV), just as our forefathers wrote about. Let us strive each day to show the world the majesty, love, and honor we have found as children of God.

Your sista in Christ,
Lisa

3He restores my soul; He leads me in the paths of righteousness For His name's sake. Psalm 23:3

ENDNOTES

1   David H. Stern, *The Complete Jewish Study Bible* (Peabody, MA: Hendrickson, 2016).

2   Henry Blackerby, Richard Blackerby, and Claude King, *Experiencing God* (Nashville: B&H, 2007).

3   "50 Facts About the Queen's Coronation," The Royal Family, accessed December 1, 2020, https://www.royal.uk/50-facts-about-queens-coronation-0.

4   Peter Morgan, creator, *The Crown*, Netflix, 2016.

5   *The Crown*, season 1, episode 5, "Smoke and Mirrors."

6   David H. Stern, "Glossary of Hebrew Words into English," in *The Complete Jewish Study Bible* (Peabody, MA: Hendrickson, 2016), 1837.

7   Jeffrey Kranz, "What's a Covenant? A Quick Definition and Overview," October 20, 2013, https://overviewbible.com/covenant/.

8   Ursula Petula Barzey, "11 Facts About Westminster Abbey," July 17, 2015, https://www.guidelondon.org.uk/blog/major-london-sites/11-facts-about-westminster-abbey/.

9   The Royal Family, "The Queen's Coronation."-

10 Jaymi Heimbuch, "20 Animals with Completely Ridiculous Names," last modified November 25, 2020, https://www.treehugger.com/animals-with-completely- ridiculous-names-4864307.

11 Linda Bloodworth-Thomason, creator, *Designing Women*, 1986–1993.

12 PBS, *The First Silent Night*, 2014.

13 Ruby Buddemeyer and Charlotte Chilton, "60 Strict Rules the Royal Family Has to Follow," December 12, 2019, https://www.marieclaire.com/culture/g4985/strict-rules-the-royal-family- has-to-follow/.

14 CBS Network, *I Love Lucy*, 1951–1957.

15 Buddemeyer and Chilton, "Rules the Royal Family Has to Follow."

16 Ariel ben-Lyman HaNaviy, "Tevilah and Mikveh," last modified February 2, 2006, https://messianicpublications.com/ariel-ben-lyman-hanaviy/tevilah-and-mikveh/.

Printed in the United States
by Baker & Taylor Publisher Services